Hampton-Brown

▶EDGE

 NATIONAL GEOGRAPHIC LEARNING

 CENGAGE Learning

Acknowledgments

Grateful acknowledgment is given to the authors, artists, photographers, museums, publishers, and agents for permission to reprint copyrighted material. Every effort has been made to secure the appropriate permission. If any omissions have been made or if corrections are required, please contact the Publisher.

Photographic Credits

Cover: Ancient Eye, Arches National Park, Utah, USA, Marsel van Oosten. Photograph © Marsel van Oosten/ squiver.com.

For product information and technology assistance, contact us at
Customer & Sales Support, 888-915-3276

For permission to use material from this text or product, submit all requests online at **www.cengage.com/permissions**
Further permissions questions can be emailed to
permissionrequest@cengage.com

National Geographic Learning | Cengage Learning
1 Lower Ragsdale Drive
Building 1, Suite 200
Monterey, CA 93940

Cengage Learning is a leading provider of customized learning solutions with office locations around the globe, including Singapore, the United Kingdom, Australia, Mexico, Brazil, and Japan. Locate your local office at **www.cengage.com/global**.

Visit National Geographic Learning online at **ngl.cengage.com**
Visit our corporate website at **www.cengage.com**

Printed in the USA.
Quad/Graphics, Versailles, KY

ISBN: 978-12857-34866 (Practice Book)
ISBN: 978-12857-34897 (Practice Book Teacher's Annotated Edition)

ISBN: 978-12857-67321 (Practice Masters)
Teachers are authorized to reproduce the practice masters in this book in limited quantity and solely for use in their own classrooms.

Printed in the United States of America
20 21 22
10 9 8

Contents

Contents, *continued*

UNIT 4

Contents, *continued*

UNIT 7

Grammar: Present Perfect Tense

Grammar: Perfect Tenses

Grammar: Participles and Participial Phrases

Proofreader's Marks

Mark	Meaning	Example
≡	Capitalize.	I love new york city.
/	Do not capitalize.	I'm going shopping at my favorite Store.
⊙	Add a period.	Mr Lopez is our neighbor.
?	Add a question mark.	Where is my black pen
!	Add an exclamation point.	Look out
＂Ｖ ＂Ｖ	Add quotation marks.	You are late, said the teacher.
∧	Add a comma.	Amy how are you feeling today?
⸲	Add a semicolon.	This shirt is nice however, that one brings out the color of your eyes.
◇	Add a colon.	He wakes up at 6 30 a.m.
⫟	Add a dash.	Barney he's my pet dog has run away.
{}	Add parentheses.	I want to work for the Federal Bureau of Investigation FBI .
=	Add a hyphen.	You were born in mid=September, right?
⩔	Add an apostrophe.	I m the oldest of five children.
#	Add a space.	She likes him alot.
⌒	Close up a space.	How much home work do you have?
∧	Add text.	My keys are on the table.
ℯ	Delete.	I am going too my friend's house.
⌃ℯ	Change text.	We have to much garbage.
∩	Transpose words, letters.	Did you see thier new car?
SP	Spell out.	Today he is turning 16 SP
¶	Begin a new paragraph.	"I win!" I shouted. "No, you don't," he said.
ital	Add italics.	The Spanish word for table is mesa. ital
u/s	Add underlining.	Little Women is one of my favorite books.

1 Are All Sentences the Same?

No. They Have Different Purposes.

Four Kinds of Sentences

1. Make a **statement** to tell something. End with a period.

   Andrea and I are friends. We know each other really well.

2. Ask a **question** to find out something. End with a question mark.

   Do you know Andrea, too? Is she your friend?

3. Use an **exclamation** to express a strong feeling.
   End with an exclamation point.

   What a surprise this is! Andrea plays hockey! I can't believe it!

4. Give a **command** to tell someone what to do. End with a period.
   For strong commands, end with an exclamation point.

   Tell me about hockey. Show me your skates. Watch out!

Start every sentence with a capital letter.

Try It

A. Read each sentence. Decide what kind of sentence it is. Write **statement**, **question**, **exclamation**, or **command**. Then write it as another kind of sentence.

1. Andrea is my best friend. _statement; Is Andrea my best friend?_ _____

   _____

2. What a good hockey player she is! _____

   _____

3. Is she the star of her team? _____

   _____

4. Take me to her hockey game. _____

   _____

B. These sentences are missing end punctuation. Edit the sentences to add punctuation.

5. I didn't know that Andrea plays hockey⊙

6. How surprised I was to find out

7. Why didn't she tell me

8. Please do not keep secrets from me

9. What else does Andrea do for fun

10. I will ask her more about that

Write It

C. What surprising information have you learned about someone you know? Complete the sentences to tell about it. Make sure you use the correct punctuation.

11. My best friend _____

12. Did you know _____

13. How shocked _____

14. Please tell _____

15. I never knew _____

D. (16–20) What don't your friends know about you? Write at least five sentences. Use a statement, a question, an exclamation, and a command.

_____

_____

_____

_____

_____

_____

② What Do You Need for a Sentence?
A Subject and a Predicate

A complete sentence has two parts: the **subject** and the **predicate**.

subject	predicate

Paula goes to school with Brett.

To find the parts in most sentences, ask yourself:

1. Whom or what is the sentence about? The answer is the **subject**. It may be one word or more than one word.

2. What does the subject do? The answer is the **predicate**. Like the subject, it may be one word or more than one word.

Sentence	Whom or What?	What Does the Subject Do?
Brett needs help in science.	Brett	needs help in science
His friend Paula notices.	His friend Paula	notices

Try It

A. Draw a line from each subject to a predicate to make a sentence.

1. Rosa ——————————————— finds the backpack under a tree.

2. Her backpack —————— looks for her backpack.

3. A classmate named Rico — has her books, homework, and keys in it.

   helps.

4. He

B. Complete each sentence with a subject or a predicate.

5. _____ The coach _____ teaches me to play basketball.

6. Craig _____ .

7. _____ shares her lunch with me.

8. The new girl _____ .

C. Answer the questions to tell about people who are your friends. Circle the subjects in your answers. Underline the predicates.

   9. Who is one of your friends? One of my friends is _____ .

 10. What do you and your friend do together? We _____ .

 11. How does your friend help you? _____

_____

D. (12–13) What makes someone a good friend? Write at least two complete sentences. Circle the subjects. Underline the predicates.

_____

_____

Edit It

E. (14–18) Edit this journal entry. Fill in the five missing subjects or predicates. The first one is done for you.

May 23

Celia has lived next door to me for two years. Never knew her before. I locked myself out of my house today. The windows and doors. Celia invited me in. Stayed with her until Mom got home. We. Now I have a new friend. Am glad.

Proofreader's Marks

Add text:

She
⌃ gave me lunch.

Do not capitalize:

We had Fun.

See all Proofreader's Marks on page ix.

③ What Is a Sentence About?
The Subject

The **complete subject** can be one word or a phrase of several words. Zoom in on the most important word. Is it a noun? A **noun** is the name of a person, place, thing, or idea.

1. **Joshua** played soccer last winter.
2. An opposing **player** kicked the ball hard.
3. The **ball** flew into Joshua's leg.
4. The **pain** was overwhelming.
5. An **ambulance** took him to the hospital.
6. The **emergency room** was quite busy.

Nouns in the Subject	
Person	Joshua player
Place	emergency room
Thing	ball ambulance
Idea	pain

Try It

A. Write a noun to complete the subject of each sentence about Joshua.

1. The emergency room ____doctor____ took X-rays.

2. Joshua's _____ was broken.

3. Now the unhappy _____ has a cast and crutches.

4. His _____ signed the cast and drew pictures on it.

5. The colorful _____ has to stay on for six weeks.

B. (6–10) Complete the paragraph. Write nouns to complete the subjects.

Joshua's soccer ____team____ felt bad for Joshua. The _____ decided to cheer him up by making him dinner. The big potluck _____ was delicious. Joshua's _____ was full of all kinds of food. His friends' _____ helped Joshua to feel a lot happier.

C. Suppose you broke your leg and your friends brought you food. Answer the questions to tell how some things would help. Circle the most important noun in the complete subject.

11. What foods would help your bones heal? _____ would help to

_____.

12. What foods would keep you warm? _____.

13. What foods would cheer you up? _____ would help me to feel a lot better.

14. What else would help with your recovery? _____

_____

D. (15–18) Accidents happen all the time. Write four sentences about accidents and their consequences. Use a different subject in each sentence.

_____

_____

_____

_____

_____

Edit It

E. Dear Joshua,

　　Thank you for visiting me at the hospital today. Your was very kind to drive you here. That broken must be a real problem for you. The make it hard to get around. The thought you did a great job, though. My just came in to check on me. He said I can go home soon. I can't wait. The is not my favorite place! Your can take good care of me at home.

Love,

Grandpa

Proofreader's Marks
Add text:
Joshua ∧ visited his grandpa at the hospital.
See all Proofreader's Marks on page ix.

4 What's the Most Important Word in the Predicate?

The Verb

- The **complete predicate** in a sentence often tells what the subject does. It can be one word or several words. The **verb** shows the action.

  My best friend **invites** me to her house.

  I **decide** to ride my bike.

- Sometimes the predicate tells what the subject has. It uses these **verbs**:

  My bike **has** a flat tire.

  I **have** a kit for patching it.

- Other times, the predicate tells what the subject is or is like. The **verb** is a form of **be**.

  All the tools **are** in my kit.

  My tire **is** not flat anymore.

  I **am** proud of myself!

Try It

A. Write a verb to complete the predicate of each sentence.

1. I _____ not that good at fixing things.

2. Usually, I _____ my dad for help.

3. This time I _____ my flat tire by myself.

4. Then I _____ to my friend Amy's house.

5. She _____ proud of me!

6. My dad _____ proud of me, too.

7. I _____ more confidence now.

B. (8–13) Complete the paragraph. Write verbs to complete the predicates.

We are in my friend's yard. A lost dog _____ into the yard. The friendly dog _____ a collar but no license tag. My friend's mom _____ not home. At first, we _____ what to do. Then we take care of the problem ourselves. We _____ the police. They eventually _____ the dog's owner.

Write It

C. Tell about a problem you had and how you solved it. Add predicates to the subjects below. Underline the verb in each predicate.

14. My problem _____.

15. To solve my problem, I _____.

16. Next, I _____.

D. (17–20) When have you surprised yourself by realizing you could do something you thought you couldn't do? Write at least four sentences. Underline the verb in each predicate.

_____

_____

_____

_____

_____

Edit It

E. (21–26) Edit the paragraph by adding verbs in the predicates. Fix the six mistakes.

I am on the train on my way to the city. The train car mechanical problems. An announcement passengers to leave the car. Some of the older passengers confused. How will they get help? I them to get to safety. The passengers grateful. I proud that I remain calm.

Proofreader's Marks

Add text:

show
I ‸ them what to do.

See all Proofreader's Marks on page ix.

5 Write Complete Sentences

Remember: You need a **subject** and a **predicate** to make a complete sentence. Often, the most important word in the subject is a **noun**. Every predicate needs a **verb**.

Subject	Predicate
My older **brother**	always **teases** me.
His **friends**	**give** me a hard time, too.
My **sister**	usually **spends** time with me.
My whole **family**	**enjoys** each other most of the time.

Try It

A. Write a subject, a verb, or a predicate to complete each sentence.

1. _____ is extremely hard tonight.

2. Usually, I _____ my homework by myself.

3. Tonight, I _____.

4. _____ is very good at math.

5. He _____ me all the time, though. I bet he won't help!

B. (6–10) Complete the subjects or predicates in this conversation between the two brothers.

James: Dan, my _____ is really hard. I don't get it.

Dan: Ah! My little _____ needs help with his homework!

James: Forget it. It _____ not too hard for me.

Dan: Hey, James, I'm just kidding around. I _____ that math. I'll help you.

James: Really? You'll help? So you _____ a pretty good big brother after all!

C. (11–14) Write your own conversation about another time when James asks Dan for help. Write one statement, one question, one exclamation, and one command. Remember to add the correct punctuation.

James: My _____ is _____

Dan: Do you _____

James: What a _____

Dan: Show me _____

D. (15–18) How do you and your siblings or friends get along? Write at least four sentences to explain. Use nouns in the subjects and verbs in the predicates.

_____

_____

_____

_____

_____

Edit It

E. (19–25) Edit the journal entry. Fix the seven mistakes by adding missing nouns, verbs, and end punctuation.

February 26

Basketball is my favorite sport. My brother and sister never play with me, though How surprised I am by this I outside shooting baskets. My big comes outside. He actually with me! Can you believe it I guess I'm pretty lucky to have Dan for a big brother after all

Proofreader's Marks

Add text:
am
I surprised.

Add a period:
We play basketball

Add a question mark:
Will you help me

Add an exclamation point:
How shocked I am

See all Proofreader's Marks on page ix.

6 What's a Plural Noun?

A Word That Names More Than One Thing

One	More Than One
A **singular noun** names one thing.	A **plural noun** names more than one thing.

Use these spelling rules for forming plural nouns.

1. To make most nouns plural, just add -**s**.

2. If the noun ends in **s**, **z**, **sh**, **ch**, or **x**, add -**es**.

3. If the noun ends in **y** after the consonant, change the **y** to **i** and add -**es**.

4. Some nouns have special plural forms.

One	More Than One
hope	hope**s**
dish	dish**es**
memory	memor**ies**
child	children
man	men
woman	women

Try It

A. (1–4) Read these nouns: **children**, **dream**, **family**, **wishes**. Which nouns are singular and which are plural? Put each noun in the correct column. Then add its other form. The first one is done for you.

Singular Nouns (one)	Plural Nouns (more than one)
child	children

B. (5–10) Write nouns from the chart to complete the paragraph.

My _____ lives in the same building as two other

_____. All of the _____ are

good friends. We share a lot of the same _____ and

_____. One _____ we all have is to

go to college. I hope it comes true for all of us.

Write It

C. How can you get to know someone well? Circle the singular noun in each question you might ask someone. Then use its plural form to answer the question.

11. What city do you like to visit? Cities I like to visit are _____.

12. What is your favorite movie? _____

13. What country would you like to visit? _____

14. Do you like the beach? _____

D. (15–18) Write at least four sentences about people you know well. Use at least two singular nouns and two plural nouns in your response.

_____
_____
_____
_____
_____

Edit It

E. (19–25) Edit the journal entry. Fix the seven mistakes with nouns.

November 4

I thought I knew my mother really well. Then she surprised me. She told me many story about her youth. Mom had a lot of hobby. She had two bicycle. She used to cycle all over the city. Sometimes she went on trip to other country. One of her wish was to cycle around the world. One of my dream is to go with her.

Proofreader's Marks

Change text:
My parents were ~~childs~~ children once.

See all Proofreader's Marks on page ix.

7 How Do You Know What Verb to Use?

Match It to the Subject.

- Use **I** with **am**.
  I **am** a volunteer.

- Use **he**, **she**, or **it** with **is**.
  It **is** a good experience for me.
  My job **is** to read to a child.
  He **is** happy to see me.

Forms of *Be*
I **am**
he, she, or it **is**
we, you, or they **are**

- Use **we**, **you**, or **they** with **are**.
  My friends **are** volunteers, too.
  They **are** volunteers at the soup kitchen.
  We **are** happy to help out. **Are** you?

Try It

A. (1–6) Write **am**, **is**, or **are** to complete the paragraph.

I _____ a volunteer at the neighborhood community center. My friend

Annie _____ a volunteer, too. She _____ quiet about her

volunteer work, though. People _____ surprised when they learn

that she is so involved. I _____ happy to share the time with her. It

_____ good to feel that we are helping out.

B. (7–12) Write **am**, **is**, or **are** to complete the interview with Annie.

Reporter: What _____ your favorite activities?

Annie: Well, I _____ always busy. Soccer _____ my
favorite sport.

Reporter: When _____ the practices for soccer?

Annie: They _____ every day after school. My volunteer work
_____ rewarding, too.

C. Complete the sentences to tell about some of your extracurricular activities. Use **am**, **is**, or **are** in each sentence.

13. I _____ busy because _____

_____.

14. My favorite activity _____.

15. Extracurricular activities _____ important because _____

_____.

D. (16–19) Write at least four sentences to tell how two of your friends spend their time after school. Use **am**, **is**, and **are**.

_____

_____

_____

_____

_____

E. (20–25) Edit the letter. Fix the six mistakes with verbs.

Dear Uncle Ted,

I am very busy these days. You would be surprised to find out how much I do after school. My theater group keeps me really busy. It are my favorite activity. The play are next weekend, so we is in rehearsals every day.

I also a volunteer at the community center. I have a part-time job, too. It am only a few hours a week, but it helps me save money for college. How busy I are these days!

Your favorite nephew,

Michael

Proofreader's Marks
Add text: We $\overset{are}{\wedge}$ busy.
Change text: Drama $\overset{is}{\underset{\wedge}{am}}$ fun.
See all Proofreader's Marks on page ix.

8 How Do You Know What Action Verb to Use?
Match It to the Subject.

- **Action verbs** tell when a subject does something, like **work**, **hike**, or **ride**. If the sentence is about one other person, place, or thing, add **-s** to the action verb.

  1. My grandparents **work** hard. **2.** Grandpa **works** at the hospital.

  3. They **volunteer**, too. **4.** Grandma **volunteers** at the library.

  5. I **hike** with my grandmother. **6.** She **hikes** in the mountains.

- If there is more than one action verb in a sentence, all verbs must agree with the subject:

  My grandparents **ride** bikes, **swim**, and **participate** in a book club.

Try It

A. Complete these sentences. Write the correct form of the verbs in parentheses.

1. The Lopezes _____*act*_____ a lot younger than they are. **(act)**

2. Mrs. Lopez _____ 80 this year. **(turn)**

3. She _____ her dogs for a long walk every day. **(take)**

4. Sometimes, they even _____ past my house! **(jog)**

5. I _____ that I'm that active when I'm 80. **(hope)**

B. Write action verbs to complete these sentences. Make sure each verb agrees with the subject.

6. Mr. Lopez _____ in his garden.

7. His seeds _____ into beautiful flowers every year.

8. Sometimes, I _____ Mr. Lopez with the hard tasks.

9. Mr. Lopez _____ at the local college, too.

10. His students _____ about plants from him.

C. Imagine that you are a volunteer at your local senior center. What activities do people do there? Complete the sentences. Use action verbs correctly.

11. That man _____.

12. Those women _____.

13. My grandfather _____.

14. The people _____ , _____ , and

_____.

D. (15–18) Write at least four sentences to tell what your older relatives do to keep active. Use action verbs correctly.

_____

_____

_____

_____

_____

E. (19–25) Edit the article from *Senior News*. Fix the seven mistakes with action verbs.

Senior Citizens Plan Trip to the City

The Holyoke Senior Citizen Center is an active place. Members comes every day to enjoy the activities. Some people take part in the daily bridge game. Other active seniors plays in the tennis league. Mr. Lopez organize trips to the city. Participating members steps onto the bus. The bus take them to the city. The tourists visits museums and shop in the stores. Then they return home and waits for next month's trip.

Proofreader's Marks

Change text: ride

People ~~rides~~ to the city.

See all Proofreader's Marks on page ix.

© National Geographic Learning, a part of Cengage Learning, Inc.

⑨ What's a Compound Subject?

It's a Subject with Two or More Nouns.

When a subject has two or more nouns joined by **and** or **or**, it is called a **compound subject**.

1. **Trumpets and trombones** are brass instruments.
2. **Joyce and Carlos** play brass instruments in the band.
3. The **oboe or** the **flutes** play a solo.
4. The **clarinet or** the **piccolo** is my favorite instrument.

How do you know what verb to use with a compound subject?

- If you see **and**, use a plural verb like **are** or **play**.

- If you see **or**, look at the last noun in the subject.
  If it is singular, use a singular verb.
  If it is plural, use a plural verb.

Try It

A. Write the correct form of the verbs to complete the sentences.

1. Carlos and his band _____play_____ really loud music.
    play / plays

2. Either the drums or the keyboard _____ the loudest of all.
    is / are

3. Mr. and Mrs. Green _____ the music hurts their ears.
    say / says

4. Each day, Mr. Green or Mrs. Suarez _____ about the noise.
    complain / complains

5. Carlos and his friends _____ to do something nice for the neighbors.
    want / wants

6. Carlos and the drummer _____ a free concert.
    arrange / arranges

7. Kids and adults _____ to hear them.
    come / comes

B. Choose words from each column to build four sentences. You can use words more than once.

The drummer or the guitarist		all day and all night.
My neighbor or my parents	complain	when the music plays.
The musician and his neighbors	dance	about putting on a free concert.
The band and my dad	agree	about the loud music.
	plays	

8. The drummer or the guitarist plays all day and all night.

9. _____

10. _____

11. _____

Write It

C. Complete each sentence so that it tells about a band. Use the correct form of the verb.

12. My friends and I _____.

13. Your friends or your parents _____.

14. The keyboard and the bass _____.

15. The singer or the drummer _____.

D. (16–20) Imagine you are in a band. Write at least five sentences to tell about your band and what it might do for the community. Use a compound subject in each sentence. Use both **and** and **or**.

_____

_____

_____

_____

_____

10 Make Subjects and Verbs Agree

Remember: The verb you use depends on your subject. These subjects and verbs go together:

Forms of *Be*	Action Verbs
I **am** strong.	I **learn** about people's strengths.
You **are** strong.	You **learn** about people's strengths.
He, she, or it **is** strong.	He, she, or it **learns** about people's strengths.
We, you, or they **are** strong.	We, you, or they **learn** about people's strengths.
My friends **are** strong.	My friends **learn** about people's strengths.
My friends and I **are** strong.	My friends and I **learn** about people's strengths.

Try It

A. Complete each sentence. Write the correct form of the verb.

1. Sometimes, I _____ to try something new.
   decide / decides

2. For example, my school _____ baseball tryouts every year.
   hold / holds

3. The athletic director or the coach _____ tryouts.
   announce / announces

4. Mom and Dad _____ I should try out.
   think / thinks

5. I _____ not sure that I'm good enough.
   is / am

B. (6–10) Write the correct form of a verb to complete each sentence.

I _____ to be on the team, though. Baseball _____ my favorite sport. My friends and my parents _____ me. My big brother _____ me practice. The team list comes out. Hooray! I _____ on the team!

C. Answer the questions about how you push your limits. Make sure your subjects and verbs agree.

11. How do you push your limits? I _____.

12. Who helps you? My _____ and my _____.

13. What is one of your strengths? One strength _____.

14. What does that strength help you learn about yourself? It _____

_____.

D. (15–18) How have you surprised yourself by pushing your personal limits? Write at least four sentences. Use simple subjects and compound subjects. Make sure the subjects and verbs agree.

_____

_____

_____

_____

Edit It

E. (19–25) Edit the journal entry. Fix the seven mistakes in subject-verb agreement.

July 12

Sometimes I really pull through for myself.

My experiences teaches me to trust myself.

If my mom need help, I wants to be there

for her. The same goes for my baseball

team. The coach or the captain give me

encouragement. We all works together.

They is sometimes surprised by what I can

accomplish. I feels the same way!

Proofreader's Marks

Change text:

We ~~knows~~ know ourselves and push ~~pushes~~ our limits.

See all Proofreader's Marks on page ix.

11 What Is a Fragment?

It's an Incomplete Sentence.

A **fragment** is a group of words that begins with a capital letter and ends with a period. It looks like a sentence, but it is not complete. A subject or a verb may be missing.

Fragments	Sentences
1. Is a big city high school.	My school is a big city high school.
2. Has thousands of kids in it.	It has thousands of kids in it.
3. Many of the students.	Many of the students hang out together.
4. My friends members of one group.	My friends are members of one group.

Try It

A. Write whether each group of words is a fragment or a sentence. If it is a fragment, add a subject or a verb. Write the complete sentence.

1. Some groups of students athletes. _____

   _____

2. Hang out together. _____

3. Another group likes math, music, and computers. _____

4. People that group is really smart. _____

   _____

B. Fix the fragments. Add a subject or a verb.

5. My friends and I friendly with all the groups.

6. Play sports.

7. I on the math team, too.

8. All of the groups.

Proofreader's Marks
Add text: The math team. meets on Fridays ^
Do not capitalize: I like Football.
See all Proofreader's Marks on page ix.

C. Answer the questions about groups in your school. Use complete sentences.

9. What groups exist in your high school? _____

_____

10. What groups are you part of? _____

_____

11. How do the groups get along with each other? _____

_____

D. (12–15) Write at least four sentences to tell what you think about different high school groups. Then read your sentences aloud. Fix any fragments that you might hear.

_____

_____

_____

_____

_____

Edit It

E. (16–20) Edit the journal entry. Fix the five fragments.

September 29

I am a new kid in this high school. At first, was really worried. My old high school had a lot of groups. Was hard to make friends there. Everyone in this school along, though. All the kids. I have many new friends. Some of them sports. Others are in the drama club. The kids are all nice to each other.

Proofreader's Marks

Add text:
Manny ^edits the student newspaper.

Do not capitalize:
I attend a School in the city.

See all Proofreader's Marks on page ix.

12 What's One Way to Fix a Fragment?

Add a Subject.

- A complete sentence has a **subject** and a **predicate**.
- To check for a subject, ask yourself:
  Whom or what is the sentence about?

Fragments	Sentences
1. Play sports.	**Athletes** play sports.
2. Have other interests, too.	**They** have other interests, too.
3. Plays football and writes for the student newspaper.	**Alex** plays football and writes for the student newspaper.

Try It

A. **Fix each fragment. Add a subject to turn the fragment into a complete sentence.**

1. Plays a musical instrument.

2. Paints on a canvas.

3. Is really good at sports.

4. Are good at more than one thing.

B. **Write whether each group of words is a fragment or a sentence. If it is a fragment, add a subject to make a sentence about José, an athlete who doesn't fit into a stereotype. Write the complete sentence.**

5. Some people think athletes are only interested in sports. _____

6. Is a really good athlete. _____

7. Plays saxophone in the jazz band, too. _____

_____

Proofreader's Marks

Add text:
Many people
∧re talented.

Do not capitalize:
I attend art 𝒮chool every
week.

See all Proofreader's Marks
on page ix.

C. Answer the questions to tell your opinions about stereotypes. Use complete sentences.

8. What is the stereotype of an athlete? An athlete _____

_____.

9. What do you think artists are like? I think artists _____

_____.

10. What do you think band members are like? I think band members _____

_____.

11. Are stereotypes usually accurate? Explain. Stereotypes _____

_____.

D. (12–15) Write at least four complete sentences about someone you know who doesn't fit a stereotype. Then read your sentences aloud. Fix any fragments.

_____

_____

_____

_____

_____

Edit It

E. (16–20) Edit this letter. Fix the five fragments.

Dear Bella,

I met a new friend today. Is a big football star. I don't like football players. Are only good at football. That's what I used to think, anyway. Now know better. John is really good at math. is on the math team with me. Get along together really well. I guess I learned a lesson about stereotypes!

Love,

Caitlin

Proofreader's Marks
Add text: are   We ^ friends.
Do not capitalize: We should not Stereotype.

13 What's Another Way to Fix a Fragment?

Add a Predicate, and Be Sure It Has a Verb.

When you write a sentence, be sure to include the verb. If you leave the verb out, the words you wrote are a **fragment**. Study the sentences in the chart.

Fragments	Sentences
1. I this information in the newspaper.	I **read** this information in the newspaper.
2. Firstborn children higher IQs than their siblings.	Firstborn children **have** higher IQs than their siblings.
3. All the children in my family smart!	All the children in my family **are** smart!

Try It

A. Fix each fragment. Add a verb to turn the fragment into a complete sentence.

1. Some people that youngest siblings are spoiled.

2. That belief one kind of stereotype.

3. That stereotype no sense to me.

4. My youngest sibling the same as the rest of us.

Proofreader's Marks

Add text:
　　are
We ⌄ smart.

See all Proofreader's Marks on page ix.

B. Write whether each group of words is a fragment or a sentence. If it is a fragment, add a verb to write a sentence about family stereotypes.

5. Marianna my youngest sister. _____

6. Some youngest siblings spoiled. _____

7. Marianna does all her chores. _____

8. My parents Marianna and me the same. _____

_____

C. Fix the fragments by adding predicates. Write sentences about family stereotypes.

9. Family stereotypes. _____

10. The oldest child. _____

11. The middle children. _____

12. Working moms. _____

D. (13–15) Write at least three sentences about stereotypes and your family.
Then read your sentences aloud. Fix any fragments you might hear.

_____

_____

_____

_____

_____

Edit It

E. (16–20) Edit this student's report about family stereotypes. Fix the five fragments.

Family Stereotypes

Some people think that dads don't help around the house. I think that is a stereotype. My dad around our house all the time. Every morning, he breakfast for me. On the weekends, he the lawn. Sometimes he dinner, too. My dad a lot of baseball on TV, too. Every family is different. I've learned not to believe in stereotypes.

Proofreader's Marks

Add text:

          is
My dad ∧ a great guy.

See all Proofreader's Marks on page ix.

14 What's One More Way to Fix a Fragment?

Combine Neighboring Sentences.

Writers may create a fragment by starting a new sentence when they shouldn't. These fragments are easy to fix. Just combine the fragment with the sentence before it.

```
      ┌──── sentence ────┐ ┌──── fragment ────┐
1.  I live in a neighborhood. That is multicultural.
    I live in a neighborhood that is multicultural.
```

```
      ┌──── sentence ────┐ ┌──────── fragment ────────┐
2.  I enjoy my neighborhood. Because I learn a lot about different cultures.
    I enjoy my neighborhood because I learn a lot about different cultures.
```

Try It

A. Combine each fragment with the neighboring sentence. Write the new sentence.

1. My parents moved to our neighborhood from Italy. When I was a baby. _____
   _____

2. My neighbors moved here from Greece. Before I started school. _____
   _____

3. We are close friends. Even though we have different backgrounds. _____
   _____

4. We have many neighbors. Who come from countries all around the world. _____
   _____

5. Every summer, the whole neighborhood gets together. And has a huge potluck dinner.
   _____
   _____

6. I love those dinners. Because I get to taste food from all around the world. _____
   _____

B. Combine the fragments with the sentences to make new sentences. You can use sentences and fragments more than once.

Sentences	Fragments
I do not pay attention to stereotypes.	And consider this neighborhood our home.
My neighbors come from different backgrounds.	Because I live in a multicultural neighborhood.
My neighbors and I live next to each other.	But are still my friends.

7. _____

_____

8. _____

9. _____

_____

Write It

C. Fix each fragment about stereotypes by combining it with a sentence. Write your new sentences.

10. Because the students come from many countries. _____

_____

11. Even though my best friend is from India. _____

_____

12. Before I tasted Chinese food. _____

_____

D. (13–15) Would you like to live in a multicultural neighborhood? Write at least three sentences to explain your reasons. Read your sentences aloud. Fix any fragments.

_____

_____

_____

_____

_____

⑮ Fix Sentence Fragments

Remember: You can fix a fragment by adding a subject or a predicate that includes a verb. Or, you can combine the fragment with another sentence.

Fragment:	Takes time to make a new friend.
Sentence:	It takes time to make a new friend.
Fragment:	People their thoughts and feelings.
Sentence:	People share their thoughts and feelings.
Fragment:	Friends don't make assumptions. Before they know each other.
Sentence:	Friends don't make assumptions before they know each other.

Try It

A. Fix the fragments. Write the new sentences.

1. Ava always purple socks. _____

2. I think she is weird. Because of her appearance. _____
_____

3. Then bump into Ava at the basketball court. _____
_____

4. She is a fantastic athlete. And is really funny, too. _____
_____

B. Change each fragment into a sentence about getting to know Ava. Write your sentences.

5. Ava and I. _____

6. Learn not to make assumptions about people. _____
_____

7. Because Ava is a lot like me. _____
_____

C. Answer the questions about getting to know people. Make sure you use complete sentences.

8. Why is it important to get to know people? It is important to get to know people because _____

_____.

9. Why shouldn't you make assumptions before you know someone? Assumptions _____

_____.

10. What is the best way to get to know someone? The best way to get to know someone is _____

_____.

D. (11–15) Write at least five sentences about getting to know a new friend. Then read your sentences aloud. Fix any fragments.

_____

_____

_____

_____

_____

Edit It

E. (16–20) Edit the paragraph. Fix the five fragments.

All around the world, people are different from one another. We shouldn't make judgments about those people. Until we meet them. It time to get to know new people. We can share our experiences. And our feelings with new acquaintances. Then get to know us. We get to know them, too. In this way, we beyond the stereotypes.

Proofreader's Marks
Delete:
I made a new friend. today.
Add text: is Her name Jen.
Do not capitalize: We are in Band together.
See all Proofreader's Marks on page ix.

✔ Capitalize Proper Nouns and Adjectives

- **Proper nouns** are capitalized because they name specific people, places, and things. Common nouns, which are general, are not capitalized.

Common Noun	Proper Noun
teacher	Mrs. Carson
city	Chicago

- **Proper adjectives**, which come from proper nouns, are also capitalized.

Proper Noun	Proper Adjective
Chicago	Chicagoan
Italy	Italian

Try It

A. Use proofreader's marks to correct the capitalization errors in each sentence.

1. When I was in third grade, my teacher, mrs. riggs, taught me how to play the piano.

2. My favorite piece to play was written by a german Composer.

3. By the time I was in sixth grade, I had also learned how to play the spanish guitar.

4. Later that year, I decided to go to the State music competition in detroit.

5. I placed second in the Piano Competition. Afterwards, dad took me to my favorite restaurant to celebrate.

6. After sixth grade, my family and I moved to los angeles.

7. In my Freshman Year, I joined the high school orchestra.

8. I discovered the Music of Aaron Copland. Now I want to be a Composer.

Proofreader's Marks

Capitalize:

He is from chicago.
          ≡

Do not capitalize:

He likes Italian Music.

See all Proofreader's Marks on page ix.

✓ Use Serial Commas Correctly

Serial commas are used to separate three or more words, phrases, or clauses written in a series. There should be a comma after each item in the series except the last one.

1. Rosa plays soccer, tennis, **and** basketball.

2. She ran down the field, kicked the ball, **and** scored the winning goal.

3. After the game, do you want to get pizza, hamburgers, **or** tacos?

Try It

A. (9–15) Edit the story. Fix the seven punctuation mistakes.

I have always loved music. My mom said that when I was just three years old, I used to bang on pots, pans and tabletops as if they were drums. As soon as Dad put on the radio, I started humming the tune drumming rhythms, and dancing along with the music.

Now that I am in high school, I play in the school orchestra. I can play the piano cello and drums. My dad is teaching me how to play the guitar. I'm going to play the guitar, piano, cello and drums, at our next school concert. I'm nervous, excited and scared, but with Mom and Dad cheering me on, I think I will do just fine.

Proofreader's Marks

Add a comma:

Today, we will study science, history, French‸ and math.

Delete:

I teach piano, guitar, and drums ⌿ to younger students.

B. Put the words in the right order. Write the sentence using the correct punctuation.

16. spend time volunteering / I play basketball / and practice piano / every week

_____

17. are Beethoven / some of / Mozart and Copland / my favorite composers

_____

✔ Check Your Spelling

Homonyms are words that sound alike but have different meanings and spellings. Spell these homonyms correctly when you proofread.

Homonyms and Their Meanings	Examples
it's (contraction) = it is; it has	**It's** fun to learn a new song.
its (adjective) = belonging to it	I play cello. I like **its** sound.
there (adverb) = that place or position	My first year **there** I joined the choir.
their (adjective) = belonging to them	**Their** music program is the best.
they're (contraction) = they are	**They're** going to the state music competition.

Try It

Proofreader's Marks

Change text:
They practice ~~they're~~ *their* skills.

A. Use proofreader's marks to correct the spelling errors in the following sentences.

18. Our school is having a talent show next month. Its sponsored by the student council.

19. Their signing up anyone who wants to be in the show.

20. It's goal is to raise money for a local family who lost there home in a fire.

21. They're are a lot of talented students in our school.

B. (22–27) Write a short paragraph about an event at your school. Use at least six homonyms in your paragraph.

_____

_____

_____

_____

_____

_____

_____

✓ Fix Run-on Sentences

A **run-on sentence** consists of two or more sentences written incorrectly as one sentence.

- To fix a run-on sentence, break it into shorter sentences. Replace the comma with end punctuation. Then start the second sentence with a capital letter.

  Incorrect: I want to learn how to play the cello, **since** I already know how to play the guitar, it should be easy to learn the cello.

  Correct: I want to learn how to play the cello. **Since** I already know how to play the guitar, it should be easy to learn the cello.

- Sometimes you can fix a run-on sentence by replacing the comma with a semicolon.

  Incorrect: I wanted to play guitar, **I** like its sound.

  Correct: I wanted to play guitar; **I** like its sound.

Try It

A. Read each sentence and write if it is a run-on or not. Fix each run-on and write the new sentence.

28. One day my dad offered to give me guitar lessons, from then on, we practiced together every evening. _____

_____

29. That same year, my teacher, Mrs. Carson, volunteered to give me piano lessons after school. _____

_____

30. Since I could already play guitar, I thought I would not have to practice much at piano, at first, I learned quickly. _____

_____

16 Is the Subject of a Sentence Always a Noun?

No, It Can Be a Pronoun.

- Use **I** when you talk about yourself.
  I saw the sign from the bus window.

- Use **you** when you talk to another person.
  Are **you** interested in volunteering?

- Use **he** when you talk about one man or one boy.
  Use **she** when you talk about one woman or one girl.
  Sorija Ramirez is a doctor.
  She tells me to come back on Tuesday.

- Use **it** when you talk about one place, thing, or idea.
  The program is starting soon. **It** will be interesting.

Subject Pronouns
Singular
I
you
he, she, it

Try It

A. Complete each sentence about someone who discovers a new interest. Use the subject pronouns **I**, **you**, **he**, **she**, or **it**.

1. Dr. Ramirez told me about her program. _____ told me how I could help.

2. She said to me, "_____ would be a great volunteer."

3. I am excited. _____ will help the patients and doctors.

4. Medicine is a good career. _____ is interesting.

B. (5–8) Write the correct pronoun to complete the sentence.

My dad didn't know I was volunteering. _____ asked about this new interest. Dr. Ramirez told me about her education. _____ explained how much school she completed. I thought about my classes this year so far. _____ will need to improve my grades. Dr. Ramirez told me she wasn't always the best student. _____ worked very hard to become a doctor.

C. Answer the questions about a new interest. Use subject pronouns.

9. In the past year, what new interest or hobby have you discovered? In the past year,

_____ have discovered _____.

10. How did you discover this interest? _____

_____

11. Who was surprised by your new interest? Why? _____

_____

D. (12–15) Write at least four sentences that tell more about your new interest or hobby. Use subject pronouns.

_____

_____

_____

_____

_____

Edit It

E. (16–20) Edit the letter. Fix the five mistakes in subject pronouns.

Dear Marissa,

Today I started volunteering at the hospital. He love it!
Dr. Ramirez introduced me to the patients. I is well liked by
everyone. Me would like her, too. Mr. Raul is one of the patients.
She is a kind man. I like helping people. want to be a doctor.
I will need to study hard in school.

Your friend,

Ella

Proofreader's Marks
Change text:
She ̶H̶e̶ is helpful.
Add text:
She ∧ told me what to study.
See all Proofreader's Marks on page ix.

17 Can a Pronoun Show "More Than One"?

Yes, It Can.

- Use **we** to talk about yourself and another person.

  Omar and I talked about our writing.
  We talked about my story.

- Use **you** to talk to one or more persons.

  You are talented, Omar.
  You are all talented writers.

- Use **they** to talk about more than one person or thing.

  The students listened to my story. **They** laughed and clapped.

Subject Pronouns	
Singular	**Plural**
I	we
you	you
he, she, it	they

Try It

A. Read the first sentence. Complete the second sentence with we, you, or they.

1. Ms. Stone leads our writing club. _____ meet every Wednesday.

2. When she read our work, she said, "_____ are all very good writers."

3. We write one story a month. _____ sometimes read our work aloud.

4. The students listened to my story. _____ liked it a lot.

5. After the meeting, Ms. Stone talked to us. She said, "_____ should publish your stories."

6. We talked about magazines that might publish our stories. _____ made a plan to send them to the magazines.

7. The other students are excited. _____ want to be published.

B. Choose words from each column to write five sentences. You may use words more than once.

We You They	give suggest should think choose	the magazine will buy it. publish your stories. ways to improve it. the magazines we like to read. me confidence.

8. The students give comments about each story. _____

9. We look at magazines together. _____

10. Ms. Stone says to us, "You should take a chance." _____

11. All of the students encourage me. _____

12. My teacher and I decide to send the story to a magazine. _____

_____

Write It

C. Answer the questions about a group that takes a chance, based on their abilities. Use **we**, **you**, or **they**.

13. What sports team or other group do you know that took a chance and succeeded?

_____ succeeded because _____.

14. How did this group take a chance? _____

15. Who was a critic of this group? _____ criticized them, but _____.

D. (16–20) Write at least five sentences that tell more about when this group took a chance. Use plural subject pronouns.

_____

_____

_____

_____

_____

18 Can a Compound Subject Include a Pronoun?

Yes, and the Pronoun Comes Last.

A **compound subject** can include nouns and pronouns joined by **and** or **or**.

1. My **teammates and** I will win this year.
2. **Parents and students** think the competition is tough.
3. The **team and** I are excited.
4. The **coach or the captain** has to help us.
5. **Tracy**, **Janine**, **or** I have to lead the team.

How do you know where to place the pronoun?

- Nouns always come before pronouns.
- The pronoun **I** always comes last.

Try It

A. Complete each sentence. Write the correct compound subject.

1. _____ think we have a small team.
   Our coach and I/I and our coach

2. Sandra and Ms. Smith work on speed. _____
   Ms. Smith and she/She and Ms. Smith
   think that speed is our best skill.

3. _____ gather extra equipment.
   The two teachers and we/We and the two teachers

4. _____ know there are few resources for us.
   Chris, the captain, and I/The captain, I, and Chris

5. _____ save a little money each week.
   Sarah, Sandra, and I/I, Sarah, and Sandra

6. Ms. Smith, _____ think having heart is more
   the captain, and I/I, and the captain
   important than resources.

B. Rewrite each sentence. Fix the compound subjects.

7. My mom, I, sister, and brother patch up the uniforms.

   _____

8. Our neighbors, we, and friends think we have a lot of potential.

   _____

9. But they or the opposing school often think we won't win.

   _____

10. She, I, or he will help with new plays.

   _____

11. We and the top two players have several strategies.

   _____

12. They, I, and Chris like to surprise the other team.

   _____

Write It

C. Answer the questions about a team or an organization that exceeded expectations. Use compound subjects.

13. How does an underdog team win? The players aren't expected to win. _____
    _____ play with less pressure.

14. How do members of the team overcome challenges? _____

15. Who thought the team would fail? _____

D. (16–20) Write at least five sentences that tell more about the team or organization that exceeded expectations. Use compound subjects.

   _____

   _____

   _____

   _____

   _____

⑲ How Do You Avoid Confusion with Pronouns?

Match the Pronoun to the Noun.

If you're not sure which **pronoun** to use, first find the **noun** it goes with. Then ask yourself:

- Is the noun a man or a woman?
  Use **he** for a man and **she** for a woman.

- Is the noun singular or plural? If plural, use **they**.

If a pronoun does not refer correctly to a noun, change the pronoun.

Incorrect: **Jesse** waits for the response. **It** feels nervous.

Correct: **Jesse** waits for the response. **He** feels nervous.

The pronouns in these sentences are correct. Do you know why?

1. **Teachers** think Jesse is irresponsible. **They** remember him in class.

2. **Jesse** makes changes. **He** also writes an essay about his goals.

Try It

A. Read the first sentence. Complete the second sentence with the correct pronoun.

1. Jesse wants to run for class president. _____ is taking it very seriously.

2. The teachers are not confident about Jesse's ability. _____ think he doesn't work hard in class.

3. Ms. Browne wants to give Jesse another chance. _____ asks him to write an essay to describe his goals.

4. Ms. Browne and the other teachers will read the essay. _____ will read it next week.

5. Mr. Shepard is the first teacher to read it. _____ thinks Jesse has a lot of talent.

6. The essay includes five goals. _____ describes Jesse's leadership.

B. Draw lines to logically connect the words in the first column with those in the second column.

7. All of the teachers have read the essay, and   They want to help him.

8. Ms. Browne and Mr. Santoro found a tutor for Jesse.   they like it.

9. Mr. Shepard talked to the other teachers.   He wants Jesse to succeed.

10. Mara will tutor him.   She will meet with him on Tuesdays.

Write It

C. Answer the questions about someone who exceeded expectations. Make sure the pronouns refer correctly to their nouns.

11. Who do you know who changed to meet a goal? _____

12. What did this person do to meet the goal? *He/She* _____.

13. Who were the critics, and what did they say? _____

D. (14–16) Write at least three sentences that tell more about someone who exceeded expectations. Make sure pronouns refer correctly to nouns.

_____

_____

_____

Edit It

E. (17–20) Edit the campaign flyer. Fix the four mistakes in pronouns.

Vote for Jesse. He is a winner!

Students believe it is a good leader. believe in him! Our school needs change. They can be better! Jesse will work for you. It can work for improvements.

Proofreader's Marks

Add text:
They
will vote for him.
∧

Change text:
She
He supports his election.
∧

See all Proofreader's Marks on page ix.

⑳ Use Subject Pronouns

Remember: The subject of a sentence can be a pronoun. A **subject pronoun** can be singular or plural.

- Use **I** when you talk about yourself.
- Use **you** to talk to one or more persons.
- Use **we** to talk about another person and yourself.
- Use **he**, **she**, **it**, and **they** to talk about other people or things.

  How do you know which pronoun to use? Look at the noun it goes with.
  1. If the noun is a man or boy, use **he**. If it is a woman or girl, use **she**.
  2. If the noun is a place or thing, use **it**. If the noun is plural, use **they**.

Try It

A. Complete each sentence with the correct subject pronoun.

1. Marisol leads the fundraising effort. _____ thinks we can do it.
   They / She

2. Our goal is to raise money for sports equipment. _____ think we can
   We / They
   sell food items.

3. Mr. Banderas will set up our booth. _____ will let us sell baked goods.
   He / It

4. The other coaches think raising money is too difficult. _____ say
   We / They
   equipment is too expensive.

B. Complete each sentence with the correct pronoun from the box.

he	it	she	they

5. All of the teams need equipment. _____They_____ need helmets.

6. Jeff leads the Saturday car wash fundraiser. _____ raises a lot of money.

7. Victoria helps at the booth. _____ sells food to customers.

8. The fundraiser is a success. _____ attracts many people to the school.

C. Answer the questions about a successful contest, competition, or fundraiser. Use subject pronouns.

9. What did this group accomplish? _____

10. Who organized the effort, and how? _____

11. What made this team or group unusual? _____

_____

12. What was the most memorable part of this group's or team's story? _____

_____

D. (13–16) Write at least four sentences about a group whose efforts were more successful than expected. Use subject pronouns correctly.

_____

_____

_____

_____

_____

Edit It

E. (17–20) Edit the letter. Fix the four mistakes in subject pronouns.

Dear Marisol:

You and your team did a great job. The school has money for equipment for next year. They can buy helmets and other equipment. Mr. Banderas, Ms. Smith, and I are amazed at your efforts. They think you did a great job. The teams are very happy. can play safely and well next year. He am very proud of you.

Sincerely,

Principal Johnson

Proofreader's Marks

Change text:
He
~~It~~ liked the fundraiser.

Add text:
She
sold pizzas.

See all Proofreader's Marks on page ix.

21 What Adds Action to a Sentence?
An Action Verb

- An **action verb** tells what the subject does. Some action verbs tell about an action that you cannot see.

  Minh **hikes** with his family.

  His father **likes** the mountains.

- Make sure the action verb agrees with its subject. Add **-s** if the subject tells about one place, one thing, or one other person.

  Minh buys a new pair of hiking boots.

  His **family camps** at the base of the mountain.

  He looks at the trail map.

  At night, **they plan** the climb to the top.

Try It

A. Write an action verb to complete each sentence.

1. Minh _____ his gear in his backpack.

2. Minh and his parents _____ a river in the morning.

3. Minh _____ a lot of water on the hike.

B. Complete each sentence about the hiking challenge. Write the correct action verb.

4. Minh's parents _____ Minh's gear.
    check / checks

5. Minh _____ to be careful on this steep climb.
    need / needs

6. He _____ up the mountain.
    climb / climbs

7. Minh _____ looking down.
    avoid / avoids

8. Minh and his parents _____ when they reach the top.
    celebrate / celebrates

C. You are going on a camping trip with your friend's family. You have never hiked in the mountains before. How do you meet this challenge? Use action verbs.

9. What do you do to prepare for the trip? I _____.

10. How do you make it over the rough terrain? I _____.

11. How do other people on the trip guide you? _____
_____

12. What does your group do when you reach the summit? We _____
_____.

D. (13–15) Write at least three sentences about your success with a great challenge. Use action verbs.

_____
_____
_____
_____

Edit It

E. (16–20) Edit the postcard. Fix the five mistakes in verbs.

Dear Mom and Dad,

We are on our way to base camp. Sarah pack the food. Her dad organize the tents. We helps plan the trip by using maps. I like the mountains. They are so beautiful. The sun shine brightly as we hike. I need to drink a lot of water here. On Wednesday, we makes the summit.

Love,

Brisa

Proofreader's Marks
Add text:
This hike challenge^s me.
Delete:
I stops to drink water.
See all Proofreader's Marks on page ix.

22 How Do You Know When the Action Happens?

Look at the Verb.

An **action verb** tells what the subject does. The tense of a verb tells when the action happens.

Earlier   Now   Later

Past ←————————————————————————————→ Future

Present Tense
want
want**s**

Use the **present tense** to talk about actions that happen now or that happen on a regular basis.

Mr. Taylor **wants** a safe neighborhood.

Alvaro **helps** the citizens.

They **meet** with their neighbors every Monday.

Try It

A. Underline the verb in the first sentence. Rewrite the sentence, using a different verb.

1. Alvaro speaks to the teenagers in the neighborhood. _____

_____

2. They prevent crime in the area. _____

3. Some people provide ideas for change. _____

4. The citizens notice less crime in the area. _____

_____

5. Alvaro explains how proud he is of the teenagers. _____

_____

6. Every day the teenagers gain something new from Alvaro. _____

_____

B. Complete each sentence with a verb from the box. Use the correct form of the action verb.

ask	buy	install	pick up	plant	receive	visit	work

7. The teens _____ garbage from the park.

8. The adults _____ the city for lights.

9. Mr. Taylor _____ lights with the funds.

10. Alvaro _____ a neighborhood sign at the corner.

11. A group of gardeners _____ flowers.

12. The neighbors _____ together to improve the area.

13. City leaders _____ the neighborhood.

14. The neighbors _____ an award for their improvements.

Write It

C. Citizens in your neighborhood want your help to improve the area. You know how to build, plant, and complete home improvement projects. How do you offer to help your neighborhood? Use present tense action verbs.

15. What do you do to help your neighborhood? I _____.

16. How do people in your neighborhood work together? They _____
_____.

17. Describe one way you work to improve your home or neighborhood. _____
_____

D. (18–20) Write at least three sentences about ways that people improve their neighborhoods. Use present tense action verbs.

_____

_____

_____

_____

23 Which Action Verbs End in -s?

The Ones That Go with *He*, *She*, or *It*

- An **action verb** in the **present tense** tells about something that happens now or on a regular basis.

- Add **-s** to the action verb if the subject tells about one place, one thing, or one other person.

    Yuri **likes** science. He **works** hard in school.

- If the verb ends in **sh**, **ch**, **ss**, **s**, **x**, or **z**, add **-es**.

    Time **passes**. He **reaches** for a new challenge.

- Do not add **-s** to the action verb if the subject is **I**, **you**, **we**, **they**, or a plural noun.

    They **need** help at the zoo. You **call** Yuri. You **tell** him about a volunteer job.

Try It

A. Write the correct present tense verb to complete each sentence.

1. Yuri _____ to become a veterinarian.
          hope / hopes

2. The local college _____ classes to become a veterinarian.
                    teach / teaches

3. Yuri's parents _____ money for college.
                save / saves

4. The college _____ a scholarship.
              offer / offers

B. Write the correct present tense form of the verb in parentheses.

5. Yuri _____ the animals at the zoo. **(watch)**

6. He _____ about how to behave around large animals. **(learn)**

7. His family _____ him to succeed. **(push)**

8. They _____ he can get the scholarship. **(think)**

C. Answer the questions about your career goals. Use present tense verbs.

9. What profession or career are you interested in? I _____
_____.

10. What do you need to study for this career? To be a _____, you _____
_____.

11. What can you do now to get ready for this career? _____
_____

12. How do your family members or teachers help you reach this goal? _____
_____

D. (13–15) Write at least three sentences about what you can do to reach your career goal. Use present tense verbs.

_____

_____

_____

_____

Edit It

E. (16–20) Edit the letter. Fix the five mistakes in verbs.

Dear Zoo Director:

    I read your ad for volunteers. I think I can do this work. Our dog up our yard. I cleans it up, and I cares for four large dogs in our neighborhood. This work disgust my friends. I don't mind. I am good with animals. You gives great care to the zoo animals. I want to help.

Sincerely,

David Brennar

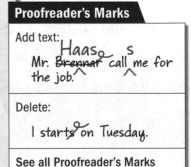

Proofreader's Marks

Add text:
Mr. Brennar call me for the job.
Haas ᵒ ˢ

Delete:
I starts on Tuesday.

See all Proofreader's Marks on page ix.

24 What Kinds of Verbs Are *Can, Could, May,* and *Might?*

They Are Helping Verbs.

- An action verb can have two parts: a **helping verb** and a **main verb**. The main verb shows the action.

  Today, Charles **walks** with a guide dog. He **may walk** into the city.

- Some helping verbs change the meaning of the action verb.

  1. Use **can** or **could** to tell about an ability.

  Charles **can walk** to many places.

  He **could walk** around in his building last month.

  2. Use **may, might,** or **could** to tell about a possibility.

  Charles **may walk** to the store. He **might visit** the museum, too.

  Charles **could walk** to the park if he has time.

- **Can, could, may,** and **might** stay the same with all subjects. Do not add -**s**.

  His dog **knows** what to do. She **can sense** danger. Charles **might enjoy** many new things with his guide dog.

Try It

A. Complete each sentence with **can, could, may,** or **might.** More than one answer is possible.

1. Charles always thought he _____ take care of a guide dog.

2. With the guide dog, he believes he _____ do anything.

3. Yesterday, they walked one-half mile. Tomorrow, they _____ walk a mile.

4. Charles _____ let the dog rest this afternoon.

5. His dog's name is Sally. She _____ help Charles get around the city.

6. Tomorrow, they _____ go to the beach.

B. Complete each sentence with the appropriate helping verb.

7. Sally is a Labrador retriever. She _____ help Charles cross streets.
   can / might

8. Charles takes care of her. He _____ brush her on Tuesday.
   could / may

9. Sally _____ change Charles's life.
   could / might

10. Sally knows how to help Charles on the bus. She _____ help him
    can / might
    board the bus.

11. Sally makes decisions near stairways. She _____ stop Charles at
    could / may
    the bottom of stairs.

12. Charles is responsible for giving commands. He _____ tell Sally
    can / could
    where to go.

13. Sally makes other decisions. She _____ decide to stop without a
    can / may
    command.

Write It

C. Answer the questions about a pet as a companion. Use the helping verbs
can, **could**, **may**, or **might**.

14. Have you ever had a pet or known a friend's pet? What can pets do? A pet _____
    _____.

15. What might a dog do to comfort you? _____

16. What could you teach a pet to do? _____

D. (17–20) Write at least four sentences about a pet you have or a friend has.
Use **can**, **could**, **may**, and **might**.

_____

_____

_____

_____

25 Use Action Verbs in the Present Tense

Remember: A verb must agree with its subject.

- Subjects **I**, **you**, **we**, **they**, or **plural nouns** do not add **-s** on the **action verb**. Subjects that tell about one place, one thing, or one other person take **-s**.

I **dream** about a goal.	Natalya **dreams** about the Olympics.
You **believe** in her goals.	She **believes** she can win a medal.
We **motivate** each other.	The competition **motivates** people.
They **ask** how they can help.	Jared **asks** Natalya about her goals.

- These verbs don't change. Do you know why?

A coach **may help** Natalya.	She **might learn** new strategies.
He **can inspire** her to win.	She **could become** a medalist.

Try It

A. Choose the correct present tense verb to complete each sentence.

1. Natalya _____ about winning a medal.
   dream / dreams

2. Jared dreams that he _____ in the major league.
   may play / may plays

3. They _____ to be the best.
   work / works

4. Their goals _____ to success.
   may lead / mays lead

B. Write the correct present tense form of the verb in parentheses.

5. Natalya _____ to train every day. **(want)**

6. Her injury _____ disappointment. **(cause)**

7. She _____ again. **(train)**

8. Natalya _____ the results of hard work. **(learn)**

9. Her medals _____ in her room. **(hang)**

C. Answer the questions about someone who doesn't give up on a dream. Use the correct form of present tense verbs.

10. Who do you know who doesn't give up, even after failure? I _____

_____.

11. What can this person do that is special? This person _____

_____.

12. What might this person do in the future? _____

_____

D. (13–15) Write at least three sentences about someone who overcame failure and became a success. Use some present tense verbs in your response.

_____

_____

_____

_____

_____

Edit It

E. (16–20) Edit the postcard. Fix the five mistakes in present tense verbs.

Dear Natalya,

   Tomorrow is the big tennis tournament! I look forward to watching you compete.

   My family like to watch you, too. They can comes with me. We are not sure, but we bring the video camera. Your dream inspire me. We knows you can make it to the Olympics!

Love,

Katie

Proofreader's Marks
Delete: I likes̸ tennis.
Add text: s She believe she can win.
See all Proofreader's Marks on page ix.

26 What Forms of *Be* Are Used in the Present?

Am, Is, and *Are*

- Use the form of the verb **be** that matches the subject.

  I **am** happy for Moni.

  She **is** the oldest child in a family of five children.

  Her sisters **are** young.

  They **are** in grade school.

  We **are** happy that Moni will go to college.

Present Tense Forms of *Be*
I **am**
he, she, or it **is**
we, you, or they **are**

- Use **not** after the **verbs am, is,** and **are** to make a sentence negative. The short form of **is not** is **isn't**. The short form of **are not** is **aren't**.

  1. Moni **is not** nervous about going to college.

     Moni **isn't** nervous about going to college.

  2. Her sisters **are not** in high school yet.

     Her sisters **aren't** in high school yet.

Try It

A. Complete each sentence with the correct form of be.

1. Moni's parents _____ proud of her.
   am / are

2. Moni _____ the first person in her family to go to college.
   am / is

3. We _____ delighted that she is going to college.
   is / are

4. You _____ happy for her, aren't you?
   am / are

5. Moni _____ worried about tough classes.
   isn't / aren't

6. She _____ committed to succeeding.
   am / is

B. Draw lines to logically connect the words in the first column to those in the second column.

7. Moni's sisters   aren't surprised by Moni's good grades.

8. Moni   is busy preparing for college.

9. All of Moni's friends   isn't registered for a local college.

10. Her teachers   are also busy preparing for college this fall.

11. She   are hopeful about going to college, too.

Write It

C. Your friend wants to do something that no one in his or her family has ever done before. Answer the questions about being the first to do something. Use present tense forms of **be**.

12. Is his or her family supportive about this dream? How? My friend's family _____
_____.

13. What do your friend's parents expect from their son or daughter? They _____
_____.

14. What is it like to be the first at something? It _____
_____.

15. Are you supportive of your friend? How? _____
_____
_____

D. (16–20) Write at least five sentences about something that you would like to be the first to do. Use present tense forms of **be**.

_____

_____

_____

_____

_____

_____

27 How Do You Show That an Action Is in Process?

Use *Am, Is,* or *Are* Plus the *-ing* Form of the Verb.

- The **present progressive** form of the verb ends in **-ing**.
- Use **am, is**, or **are** plus a **main verb** with **-ing** to show that an action is in the process of happening. The **helping verb** must agree with the subject.

  I **am helping** Ms. Torre.
  The group **is learning** how to save water.
  They **are learning** how much water these plants need.
  Ms. Torre **is teaching** us to use different plants to save water.

Try It

A. Complete each sentence. Write the correct present progressive verb form.

1. Ms. Torre _____ a garden that needs very little water.
   am designing / is designing

2. She _____ us how to use plants that grow well here.
   are showing / is showing

3. The neighbors _____ flowers that can survive without rain.
   is planting / are planting

4. I _____ a plan for the tall grass plants that will improve the area.
   am following / are following

5. These plants _____ the prairie land that existed years ago.
   is recreating / are recreating

B. Complete each sentence. Write the present progressive form of the verb in parentheses.

6. I _____ plants that will conserve water. **(discover)**

7. Ms. Torre _____ the city money with these plants, too. **(save)**

8. She _____ new techniques with the city planners. **(share)**

9. The plants _____ in a healthy way. **(grow)**

10. They _____ the city park with beauty. **(fill)**

C. You want to improve the environment. What is your plan to help save water and trees, or to recycle? Use present progressive verb forms.

11. What are you doing in your school or neighborhood to help the environment? I _____

_____ .

12. How are people in your area trying to help the environment? _____

_____

13. Describe an animal or a plant that is in danger of becoming extinct. What are people doing to help change this situation? _____

_____

D. (14–16) Write at least three sentences about ways that people are improving the environment. Use present progressive verb forms.

_____

_____

_____

_____

_____

Edit It

E. (17–20) Edit the community flyer. Fix the four errors in present progressive verb forms.

Logan Square Garden Club is learning about water!

You going to help us save water.

We are give classes on Saturday. We am teaching about good plants for our area.

You are help your town if you conserve.

Proofreader's Marks
Add text:
are
You ⌃ saving water.
Change text:
ing
I am hope that you will help. ⌃
See all Proofreader's Marks on page ix.

28 What Forms of *Have* Are Used in the Present?

Have and Has

Use the form of the verb **have** that matches the subject.

- I **have** a copy of the magazine.
- Do you **have** this fabric?
- Maritza **has** a sewing machine.
- She **has** a book of designs.
- Designers **have** a lot of ideas.
- We all **have** different styles.

Present Tense Forms of *Have*
I **have**
he, she, or it **has**
we, you, or they **have**

Try It

A. Complete each sentence with the correct form of have.

1. Maritza _____ a lot of fashion magazines.
   have / has

2. Do you _____ a copy of the September issue?
   have / has

3. Maritza _____ a new way to make her designs.
   have / has

4. Now she _____ a plan to use her sewing machine.
   have / has

B. Complete each sentence with have or has.

5. We _____ an idea for Maritza about the fashion design group.

6. The fashion designers _____ a lot of experience.

7. One fashion buyer _____ an interest in Maritza's work.

8. Maritza's designs _____ a unique look.

C. Answer the questions about reaching a goal. Use present tense forms of **have**.

9. What talent or skill do you have that you would like to develop? _____

_____

10. Who do you know who can inspire and motivate you? _____

_____

11. What resources do you have that will help you along the way? _____

_____

12. What do other people have that will help you face the challenge? _____

_____

D. (13–16) Write at least four sentences about a hero or role model who has inspired you. Use present tense forms of **have** in some of your sentences.

_____

_____

_____

_____

_____

Edit It

E. (17–20) Edit the letter. Fix the four errors with **have** and **has**.

Dear Uncle Martin,

   Mom has a photo album with pictures of you. It have several pictures of you at the top of mountains you climbed. She have pride in your achievements as a mountain climber. You a lot of courage to climb those peaks. Thanks to you, I am inspired to go after my dreams. I has a desire to become a climber, too.

Andrew

Proofreader's Marks

Add text:
You ∧ a goal to rock climb.
have

Change text:
Pedro ~~have~~ the right gear for you.
has

See all Proofreader's Marks on page ix.

㉙ What Forms of *Do* Are Used in the Present?

Do and Does

- Use the form of **do** that matches the subject. You can use **do** as a **main verb** or as a **helping verb**.

  Jorge **does** three sports during the week.

  We **do** admire him.

  Our workouts **do** help us.

  They **do** prepare our bodies for the competition.

  We always **do** our best.

Present Tense Forms of *Do*
I **do**
he, she, or it **does**
we, you, or they **do**

- The short form of **does not** is **doesn't**.

- The short form of **do not** is **don't**.

  1. He **does not** accept failure.

     He **doesn't** accept failure.

  2. They **do not** expect him to win.

     They **don't** expect him to win.

Try It

A. Complete the sentence with the correct form of **do**.

1. Jorge _____ his workout routine every day.
   do / does

2. His friends _____ some of the exercises with him.
   do / does

3. They _____ work out every day.
   doesn't / don't

4. Jorge _____ miss a day.
   doesn't / don't

5. We _____ admire how he pushes himself.
   do / does

6. Jorge _____ enjoy this new challenge.
   do / does

7. The training is intense, but it _____ bother him.
   doesn't / don't

B. Complete the sentence with **do**, **does**, **don't**, or **doesn't**.

8. Jorge _____ fifty push-ups every morning.

9. He _____ his strength training every day after school.

10. The biking _____ worry him because the course is easy.

11. The swimming _____ tire him after so many laps.

12. Jorge's coach _____ want him to injure himself.

13. Since he started this challenge, Jorge's teachers _____ think he is the same person.

14. Jorge _____ enjoy this new way of testing his abilities.

15. We _____ hope he wins the event.

Write It

C. Answer the questions about challenging yourself. Use **do** and **does** in some of your sentences.

16. What do you do to push yourself to exceed expectations? I _____

_____.

17. What do you do to prepare for the challenge? _____

_____

18. What do other people do to help you? _____

_____

D. (19–20) Write at least two sentences about how you test your abilities and push yourself to succeed. Use present tense forms of **do**.

_____

_____

_____

_____

30 Use Verbs to Talk About the Present

Remember: The verbs **be**, **have**, and **do** each have more than one form in the present. Use the form that goes with the subject.

Forms of *Be*	Forms of *Have*	Forms of *Do*
I **am**	I **have**	I **do**
he, she, or it **is**	he, she, or it **has**	he, she, or it **does**
we, you, or they **are**	we, you, or they **have**	we, you, or they **do**

Try It

A. **Complete the sentence. Write the correct form of the verb.**

1. I _____ reading a book about an explorer.
   am / is

2. He _____ famous for traveling to Antarctica.
   are / is

3. The explorer and his crew _____ many adventures along the way.
   have / has

4. I _____ a dream to become an explorer, too.
   have / has

B. **Complete each sentence with the correct present tense form of the verb in parentheses.**

5. I _____ like to travel to unusual places. **(do)**

6. An explorer _____ a life of adventure. **(have)**

7. In the book, the crew _____ an accident. **(have)**

8. I _____ understand that a journey can be dangerous. **(do)**

9. We _____ a lot to learn from modern explorers. **(have)**

Write It

C. You admire a person for something he or she does that makes a positive change in the world. What can you do to honor this person? Answer the questions. Use present tense forms of the verbs **be**, **have**, or **do** in some of your sentences.

10. What does this person do that inspires you? _____

_____

11. What qualities and experience does this person have that make you admire him or her?

_____

12. What are you doing now to honor what this person does? _____

_____

D. (13–16) Write at least four sentences about someone you admire. Use present tense forms of the verbs **be**, **have**, or **do** in some of your sentences.

_____

_____

_____

_____

_____

Edit It

E. (17–20) Edit the postcard. Fix the four mistakes in verb forms.

Dear Natalie,

    I am eager to meet the explorer this weekend at the book signing. As you know, his writings is an inspiration to me. He do not let fear get in the way of his goal. I already has a copy of his latest book. I know that you has great respect for this man, too. I will meet you at the bookstore.

See you soon,

Brigitte

Proofreader's Marks

Change text:
have
I ~~has~~ a new book.
^

See all Proofreader's Marks on page ix.

✔ Capitalize Job Titles, Courtesy Titles, and Family Titles

- **Job titles** should be capitalized when they come before a person's name. When they follow the person's name or the word **the**, they are not capitalized.

  Coach Jones

  Mr. Jones, **the coach**

  Mr. David Jones is **the coach**.

- **Courtesy titles**, such as **Mr.**, **Mrs.**, and **Ms.** should always be capitalized.

  Mr. Santoro's rules

  Ms. Hansen's class

- **Family titles** should be capitalized when they are used in place of a person's name. When they follow a possessive adjective, they are not capitalized.

  I helped **Dad** pack the car for our trip.

  I helped **my dad** pack the car for our trip.

Try It

A. Use proofreader's marks to correct the capitalization error in each sentence.

1. Our high school soccer coach is mr. Turner.

2. I asked coach Turner if I could try out for the soccer team.

3. The Principal, Ms. Morgan, took me to the soccer field.

4. I saw mom after tryouts and told her the good news.

5. My Dad was excited to hear that I made the team.

Proofreader's Marks
Capitalize:
This is principal Mendez. ≡
Do not capitalize:
Dr. Mendez is the ⫻rincipal.
See all Proofreader's Marks on page ix.

✓ Use the Dash Correctly

- Use a dash or pair of dashes to show a sudden change in thought or speech.

  They got me a magazine that's all about—**you guessed it**—soccer.

- Do not overuse dashes. For example, dashes should not be used in place of periods, commas, and other appropriate punctuation.

  Incorrect: I nodded—ran onto the field—and found the team captain.

  Correct: I nodded, **ran onto the field**, and found the team captain.

Try It

A. (6–10) Edit the journal entry. Find and fix the five punctuation mistakes.

October 20

Today was the day of the big game. No one   not even the principal   thought we'd make it this far. I couldn't believe it   the state championships! I put on my uniform — grabbed my water bottle —and headed out to the field. All eyes were on us. We were here to win, but we also knew that trying our best was the real win.

Proofreader's Marks

Add a dash:

Suddenly, I saw what it was—a soccer ball.

Replace dashes:

Next, I took a deep breath.

B. Rewrite each sentence using a dash or pair of dashes.

11. Mr. Turner he's the soccer coach let me try out.

_____

12. I ran down the field with the ball passing everyone and kicked the ball right into the net.

_____

_____

✔ Check Your Spelling

Homonyms are words that sound alike but have different meanings and spellings. Spell these homonyms correctly when you proofread.

Homonyms and Their Meanings	Examples
to (preposition) = toward, in the direction of	I am going **to** soccer tryouts.
two (noun) = one more than one	I scored **two** goals.
too (adverb) = also	Do you want to play soccer, **too**?
your (adjective) = belonging to you	Can you show us **your** soccer skills?
you're (contraction) = you are	**You're** going to be late for tryouts.

Try It

A. Complete each sentence. Use the correct homonym.

13. On the way _____ tryouts, the family car broke down.
to / two / too

14. We waited _____ hours for a tow truck.
to / two / too

15. " _____ going to be late for the tryouts," my mother said.
Your / You're

16. After what seemed liked hours, we finally made it _____ the school.
to / two / too

B. (17–19) Write a short paragraph about an obstacle or challenge that you overcame. Use at least three homonyms in your paragraph.

_____

_____

_____

_____

_____

✓ Use the Verbs *Can*, *Could*, *May*, and *Might* Correctly

- Use **may**, **might**, or **could** to tell about a possibility.
  We **might win** the championship.
  We **may** be the next champions!
  We **could become** the best team in the state.

- Use **may** to tell that an action is permitted, or allowed.
  Coach said, "If you finish your laps, you **may leave**."

- Use **can** or **could** to tell about an ability.
  Melissa **can kick** the farthest.
  She **could kick** well last year, too.

Try It

A. (20–25) Complete the story with **can**, **could**, **may**, and **might**.

   I'll never forget that day when I auditioned for the Paul Robeson School of the

Performing Arts. I thought I _____ get admitted to the program, but

I wasn't sure. I was nervous. Sure, I _____ speak two languages, but

in that first moment on stage, I _____ not remember a syllable of

either one.

   "You _____ begin now, Anthony," Ms. Gupta said. I looked up

and saw a row of teachers waiting for me to begin. Then I remembered what

my teacher Mrs. Rico always said. She said, "Whenever you get nervous, you

_____ want to take a deep breath." So I cleared my throat and took

a deep breath. Ever since I was old enough to talk, I _____ act. This

is what I love to do! I started to speak, and my nervousness slowly disappeared.

Finally, I bowed.

   That day, I overcame my stage fright—and I got admitted to the school!

31 How Do You Show That an Action Already Happened?

Add -ed to the Verb.

- Action in the **present tense** happens now or on a regular basis.
- Action in the **past tense** happened earlier.

Past ⟵ Earlier ● ··· Now ● ··· Later ○ ⟶ Future

Past Tense
played

Present Tense
play, plays

Add **-ed** to most verbs when you talk about a past action. If there is more than one verb in a sentence, they must all be in the same tense.

1. Linh and Jess **play** music together. They **played** in a concert yesterday.

2. They often **encounter** new songs, **learn** them, and **play** them. They **encountered** one, **learned** it, and **played** it last week.

Try It

A. Complete each sentence. Write the past tense of each verb in parentheses.

1. The director of the youth orchestra _____ a poster. **(display)**

2. The orchestra _____ new members. **(need)**

3. The director _____ musicians to audition. **(want)**

4. Linh and Jess both _____ and _____ at the poster. **(look) (talk)**

5. They _____ trying out and decided to do so. **(discuss)**

B. Write the present tense or past tense of the verb in parentheses.

6. Earlier this morning, Linh and Jess _____ to the tryouts. **(walk)**

7. A few hours ago, they both _____ for the orchestra. **(audition)**

8. They _____ very well and were proud of themselves. **(perform)**

C. Imagine that two friends ran against each other for student council president. One won, and the other lost. Write sentences about what probably happened after the election. Use the past tense of the verb in parentheses.

9. **(talk)** They probably _____.

10. **(learn)** They _____.

11. **(remain)** They _____.

D. (12–15) Write at least four sentences to tell about a time when you and a friend worked together and when you worked against each other. Use past tense verbs that end in -ed. In one sentence, use three past tense verbs.

_____

_____

_____

_____

_____

Edit It

E. (16–20) Edit the journal entry. Fix five mistakes with verbs.

May 10

Right now, I really need to find a job.

Yesterday, I filled out an application. The job

sound interesting. My best friend applied for

the same job! That was not good! Earlier

this morning, the managers call my friend

and offer him the job. A few minutes ago,

we talk about it. We're still friends, but I

still needed to find a job.

Proofreader's Marks

Change text:

Yesterday, I want that job. (wanted)

See all Proofreader's Marks on page ix.

32 Can You Just Add -ed to Form a Verb in the Past?

Not Always

> Most verbs end with **-ed** to show the past tense. Sometimes you have to change the spelling of the verb before you add **-ed**. Follow these rules:
>
> 1. If a verb ends in silent **e**, drop the **e**. Then add **-ed**.
>   Josh decid**ed** to play for the Blazers. **(decide)**
>   Scott's team compet**ed** against the Blazers. **(compete)**
>
> 2. Some one-syllable verbs end in one vowel and one consonant. Double the consonant before you add **-ed**.
>   Josh and Scott jog**ged** together. **(jog)**
>   Then they bat**ted** the ball around. **(bat)**

Try It

A. Complete each sentence. Write the past tense of the verb in parentheses.

1. Scott and Josh _____ about the big game. **(joke)**

2. Each boy _____ his team would win. **(hope)**

3. They _____ each other on the back. **(pat)**

4. They even _____ at each other. **(grin)**

5. Then the boys _____ and joined their own teams. **(wave)**

B. (6–10) Complete each sentence. Choose a verb from the box and use its past tense form.

grab	raise	slug	smile	tag

Josh _____ the bat into position. He _____ the ball.

Then Scott _____ it. Scott _____ Josh out at first base.

Scott _____ because his team won the game.

C. Answer each question about competing against a friend. Use the past tense.

11. When did you compete against a friend? I _____.

12. How did the competition end? _____

13. Did you like the competition? _____

14. What did you and your friend plan to do next? _____

D. (15–18) Imagine that two friends competed against each other in a game of basketball. Write at least four sentences about the competition. Use the past tense of these verbs: **dribble, move, clap, drop.**

_____

_____

_____

_____

_____

Edit It

E. (19–25) Edit this letter. Fix seven mistakes with verbs.

Dear Scott,

   Do you remember that last game we played before I move? I loveed playing against your team. I line out to you, but I also tag you out! Do you remember when Ross droped that fly ball? We ussed to have a lot of fun, didn't we? I miss those days. I am sorry I moveed away.

Your friend,

Josh

Proofreader's Marks

Change text:

competed
We ~~competed~~ well.
        ^

See all Proofreader's Marks on page ix.

33 When Do You Use *Was* and *Were*?

When You Tell About the Past

The verb **be** has special forms to tell about the present and the past.

Earlier	Now	Later
Past ⟵ ●	●	○ ⟶ Future

Past Tense	**Present Tense**
I **was**	I **am**
you **were**	you **are**
he, she, or it **was**	he, she, or it **is**
we **were**	we **are**
they **were**	they **are**

Present: Josie **is** at Alberto's party.

Past: She **was** not there last year.

Present: Josie and Alberto **are** good friends now.

Past: They **were** not good friends last year.

Try It

A. **Rewrite each sentence. Use the past tense of the verb.**

1. I am Josie's good friend. _____

2. Josie and Alberto are good friends. _____

3. Alberto is not my friend. _____

4. Josie is one of the kids invited to Alberto's party. _____

_____

5. I am not on the guest list. _____

B. Complete each sentence. Write **was**, **were**, or **are**.

6. Last week, my feelings _____ hurt.

7. Then Josie _____ thoughtful of my feelings.

8. Her friends _____ thoughtful, too.

9. They _____ nice when they talked to Alberto.

10. He _____ happy to invite me to his party.

11. I _____ glad to be invited.

12. Now Alberto, Josie, and I _____ all good friends.

Write It

C. Complete the sentences to tell about a time you felt left out. Use **was** or **were** in each sentence.

13. I _____.

14. My friends _____.

15. We all _____.

16. It _____.

D. (17–20) Write at least four sentences to tell about a time a friend of yours was left out. What did you do? Use **was** or **were** in each sentence.

_____

_____

_____

_____

_____

34 When Do You Use *Had*?

When You Tell About the Past

The verb **have** uses special forms to show the present and the past.

Past Tense	Present Tense
I **had**	I **have**
you **had**	you **have**
he, she, or it **had**	he, she, or it **has**
we **had**	we **have**
they **had**	they **have**

Present: Brad **has** a problem.   **Past:**   He **had** a bad day yesterday.

Present: Brad and Tony **have** a choice to make today.

Past: They **had** a choice to make yesterday, too.

Try It

A. Rewrite each sentence. Use the past tense of the verb.

1. Brad and Tony have a great friendship. _____

_____

2. They accidentally damage some school property on Monday. _____

_____

3. On Tuesday, the principal has Tony in his office. _____

_____

4. Tony has a chance to protect Brad. _____

_____

B. Write **have** or **has** to complete each sentence. Then rewrite the sentence in the past tense.

5. Brad _____ a strong sense of loyalty to his friend.

_____

6. He _____ a tough decision to make.

_____

7. His parents _____ some advice for him.

_____

8. Brad _____ good advice.

_____

9. Brad and Tony _____ detention together for a week.

_____

Write It

C. Complete the sentences to tell about a time you had a decision to make. Use the past tense of **have** in each sentence.

10. I _____

_____.

11. My friends _____

_____.

12. We _____

_____.

D. (13–15) Write at least three sentences about loyalty to friends. Use **have**, **has**, and **had**.

_____

_____

_____

_____

_____

35 Use Verb Tenses

Remember: You have to change the verb to show the past tense.
Be sure to use the same tense for all verbs in the same sentence.

Add **-ed** to most verbs. You may need to make a spelling change before you add **-ed**.

Present Tense	Past Tense
look, looks	looked
want, wants	wanted
hop, hops	hopped
use, uses	used

Use special forms for the past tense of **be** and **have**.

Forms of Be

Present Tense	Past Tense
am, is, are	was, were

Forms of Have

Present Tense	Past Tense
have, has	had

Try It

A. Write the correct form of the verbs to complete the sentences.

1. Last week, the teacher _____ Ana and Jo to judge the art contest.
   ask / asked

2. By the end of the week, the girls _____ to decide what to do.
   have / had

3. Right now, they _____ judges.
   are / were

4. A few days ago, their friends _____ their art in the contest.
   enter / entered

5. Afterward, their friends _____ about being friends with the judges!
   joke / joked

B. Complete each sentence. Write the past tense of the verb in parentheses.

6–7. Ana and Jo _____ and _____ to be fair. **(need) (hope)**

8. They _____ over all the artists' names. **(skip)**

C. Complete the sentences to tell about a contest in which students had to choose between loyalty and fairness. Use the past tense of the verbs in parentheses.

9. **(judge)** Students _____.

10. **(be)** The contest _____.

11. **(have)** Everyone _____.

12. **(grin)** The winner _____.

D. (13–16) Write at least four sentences about a time you had to choose between loyalty and fairness. Use past tense verbs, including the past tense of **be** and **have**, in your sentences. In one sentence, use three past tense verbs.

_____

_____

_____

_____

_____

_____

E. (17–25) Edit the student newspaper article about the art contest. Fix eight mistakes with verbs.

Art Contest Winners Chosen

Last week, our school sponsored an art contest. All the students has a chance to enter. The art teachers invitted students to judge the contest. The student judges was fair. They pushhed aside their loyalty to their friends and base their decisions on the quality of the art. The teachers snaped this photo of the judges and winners. The contest is a success. The winners was happy and smiles to show it..

Proofreader's Marks

Change text:
$$\text{was}$$
I ~~were~~ a judge in the
art show.

See all Proofreader's Marks on page ix.

36 How Do You Show That an Action Already Happened?

Change the Verb.

Add **-ed** to most verbs to show that an action already happened.
Use special past tense forms for **irregular verbs**.

Present	Past	Example in the Past
am, is, are	was, were	Susan **was** a piano teacher.
say	said	My friend **said** she was a good teacher.
do, does	did	She **did** a great job teaching him to play.
have, has	had	My friend **had** fun studying with Susan.
wake	woke	He **woke** up every morning and practiced.
hear	heard	Sometimes I **heard** him from next door.
ring	rang	When my alarm clock **rang**, I was already awake.

Try It

A. **Rewrite each sentence. Use the past tense of the verb.**

1. Susan hears about a job at the music store. _____

_____

2. She is a great candidate for the job. _____

_____

3. Susan has years of teaching experience. _____

_____

4. My friend rings up the store on the telephone. _____

_____

5. He says that she would be a great teacher. _____

_____

B. Complete each sentence with the past tense of a verb from the box.
Use **be** two times.

be	do	have	hear	ring	say	wake

6. The telephone at Susan's house _____.

7. Susan _____ it from outside.

8. The manager at the music store _____ bad news for her.

9. He _____ someone else got the job.

10. That applicant _____ a friend of the manager.

11. The call _____ Susan up to the realities of life.

12. Susan _____ everything she could.

13. _____ things fair when a friend of the manager got the job?

Write It

C. Answer the questions to give your opinions about Susan's situation. Use the
past tense of irregular verbs.

14. What loyalties did the store manager have? The store manager _____

_____.

15. Was what happened to Susan fair? _____

_____

16. What do you think Susan said to the manager? _____

_____

D. (17–20) Write at least four sentences to tell how loyalties helped you or kept
you from getting something you wanted. Use the past tense of at least four
irregular verbs.

_____

_____

_____

_____

37 How Do You Show That an Action Already Happened?

Change the Verb.

Add **-ed** to most verbs to show that an action already happened.
Use special past tense forms for **irregular verbs**.

Present	Past	Example in the Past
feel	felt	Carlos **felt** sad when Oscar ignored him on the basketball court.
go, goes	went	Carlos and Oscar **went** to school together.
get	got	Carlos **got** a strange feeling from Oscar whenever he saw him.
know	knew	He **knew** that Oscar wasn't being nice.
meet	met	Recently, Carlos **met** Eduardo.
tell	told	Eduardo **told** Carlos about a good movie.
see	saw	The boys **saw** the movie together.

Try It

A. Complete each sentence. Write the past tense form of the verb in parentheses.

1. Carlos _____ that something was wrong. **(know)**

2. Oscar _____ him and didn't say hello. **(see)**

3. Oscar _____ off with some new friends. **(go)**

4. Carlos _____ the message. **(get)**

5. He _____ Eduardo that old friends were not always loyal friends. **(tell)**

B. (6–12) Complete the paragraph with past tense verbs.

Carlos _____ that Eduardo was a better friend than Oscar.
Even though he only _____ Eduardo a few weeks ago, Carlos
_____ closer to him. Carlos and Eduardo _____ each other
a lot. They _____ each other their problems and helped each other
out. They _____ along better than Carlos and Oscar. Carlos and Oscar
_____ their separate ways. Carlos learned that old friends were not
always best friends.

Write It

C. Answer the questions to tell about a time when an old friend was not a good friend. Use the past tense of irregular verbs.

13. What did your friend tell you? My friend _____
_____.

14. How did you feel? I _____
_____.

15. What did you know? I _____
_____.

16. Where did you go? I _____
_____.

D. (17–20) Write at least four sentences that tell about an old friend and a new friend. Use the past tense of at least four irregular verbs from the chart on page 81.

_____

_____

_____

_____

_____

38 How Do You Show That an Action Was in Process?

Use *Was* or *Were* Plus the *-ing* Form of the Verb.

- Sometimes you want to show that an action was happening over a period of time in the past. Use the past progressive form.

- To form the past progressive, use the helping verb **was** or **were** plus a main verb that ends in **-ing**. The helping verb must agree with the subject.

  Julio **was** standing outside the restaurant.
  Inside, the waiter **was** serving a customer.
  Other people **were** sitting patiently.
  They **were** becoming impatient, though.

Try It

A. Complete each sentence. Write the past progressive form of the verb in parentheses.

1. Julio _____ out the new restaurant. **(try)**

2. He _____ the food would taste really good. **(hope)**

3. Many customers _____ to be seated. **(wait)**

4. Two of the owner's friends _____ in at the restaurant. **(stop)**

5. The owner _____ them right away. **(seat)**

B. Choose a verb from the box to complete each sentence. Use the past progressive form.

| begin   feel   ignore   leave |

6. Julio _____ angry.

7. Some people _____ the line to go somewhere else to eat.

8. One customer _____ to complain.

9. The owner _____ his complaints.

C. Imagine that you were waiting in line at the restaurant. Answer the questions about your experience. Use the past progressive form of verbs in your answers.

10. What were you doing while you were waiting? _____

_____

11. How were you feeling when the owner's friends were seated first? _____

_____

12. Was the owner treating anyone fairly? What was he doing? _____

_____

D. (13–16) Write at least four sentences about a time you were treated either fairly or unfairly at a store or a restaurant. Use the past progressive form of a verb in each sentence.

_____

_____

_____

_____

_____

E. (17–20) Edit the restaurant review below. Fix four past progressive verbs.

Danny's Fish Fry

I ate at the fish restaurant last night—Danny's Fish Fry. The experience was a huge disappointment. The food was good, but the service was not. The owner was giving preferential treatment to some customers. New customers were get angry. They looking at their watches. These customers was wish they had eaten someplace else. Other customers was waiting to be served their meals. It is important to treat loyal customers well, but it is important to treat new customers well, too!

Proofreader's Marks

Add text:
                were
We⋀hoping for a good
meal.

Change text:
              was snubbing
The owner ~~were snub~~ us.
                       ⋀

See all Proofreader's Marks on page ix.

39 How Do You Tell About the Future?

Use *Will* Before the Verb.

- The **future tense** of a verb shows that an action will happen later.

Earlier   Now   Later

Past ◄────── ○ ──────── ○ ──────── ● ──────► Future

Future Tense

To form the future tense, use **will** before the main verb.

    Tim **will move** to a neighboring town.

You can also use **am**, **is**, or **are** plus **going to** before the main verb.

    He **is going to make** new friends.

If **will** or **am**, **is**, or **are** plus **going to** comes before the first verb in a series, all three verbs are in the future tense.

    He **is going to keep** his old friends, **make** new ones, and **enjoy** them all.

Try It

A. Write the future tense of the verb in parentheses to complete each sentence. More than one answer is possible.

1. Tim _____ close to his new school. **(live)**

2. His old friends _____ him in his new home. **(visit)**

3. Tim _____ back to see them, too. **(drive)**

4. Tim _____ to know new friends, too. **(get)**

5. He _____ to have friends in his new school. **(want)**

B. Write a future tense verb to complete each sentence.

6. Tim _____ loyal to his old friends and _____ them often.

7. He _____ them to his new friends.

Write It

C. Imagine that you are going to move to a new town and go to a new school. Answer the questions. Use future tense verbs.

8. How will you meet new friends? I _____.

9. How will you stay loyal to old friends? I _____.

10. Why will new friends want to know you? They _____

_____.

D. (11–12) Now write at least two sentences to tell about something you will do with your friends. Use a future tense verb in each sentence. Use three future tense verbs in one of your sentences.

_____

_____

_____

_____

Edit It

E. (13–20) Edit the journal entry. Fix eight mistakes with verbs. There is more than one way to make each correction.

May 16

Tomorrow I will have a good time. I got together with my friends. We will on a long hike together. Both my old friends and my new friends hike with me. We climbed to the top of a mountain and will view the valley. Then, we eat a picnic lunch. I enjoyed the day because all my loyal friends had fun together.

Proofreader's Marks

Add text:
    take
I will plenty of water with me.

Change text:
    will go
Tomorrow, I went on a hike.

See all Proofreader's Marks on page ix.

40 Use Verb Tenses

Remember: You have to change the verb to show when an action happens. The action can happen in the **present**, **past**, or **future**.

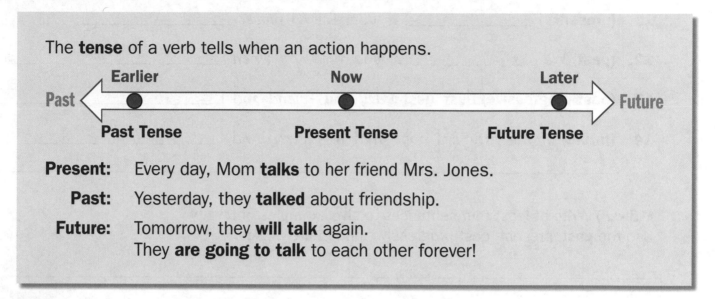

The **tense** of a verb tells when an action happens.

Earlier   Now   Later

Past ◄──────●──────────●──────────●──────► Future

Past Tense   Present Tense   Future Tense

Present: Every day, Mom **talks** to her friend Mrs. Jones.

Past: Yesterday, they **talked** about friendship.

Future: Tomorrow, they **will talk** again.
They **are going to talk** to each other forever!

Try It

A. Complete each sentence. Write the correct tense of the verb in parentheses.

1. Mom _____ Mrs. Jones years ago. **(past of meet)**

2. They _____ to kindergarten together. **(past of go)**

3. Now, Mrs. Jones _____ a new home that is far away. **(present of have)**

4. She _____ still Mom's loyal friend, though. **(present of be)**

5. Just yesterday, Mom _____ me about the friendship. **(past progressive of tell)**

6–7. She _____ that Mrs. Jones _____ us later this year. **(past of say; future of visit)**

B. Complete each sentence. Write a verb in the tense in parentheses.

8. Yesterday, I _____ my loyal friend Jenna and _____ fun. **(past)**

9. We _____ our bicycles together. **(past progressive)**

10. I hope that Jenna and I _____ loyal friends forever. **(future)**

C. Complete the sentences about a loyal friend. Use the verb tenses given in parentheses.

11. **(present)** I _____ a loyal friend named _____.

12. **(past)** We _____ a long time ago when _____.

13. **(past progressive)** Just yesterday, my friend and I _____.

14. **(future)** In the future, I hope that my friend and I _____

_____.

D. (15–18) Write at least four sentences to give examples of loyalty.
Use the past, present, past progressive, and future tenses.

_____

_____

_____

_____

_____

Edit It

E. (19–25) Edit the letter below. Fix seven mistakes.

Dear Amanda,

  Yesterday, Marie was asking about our long and loyal
friendship. I told her about how we meet when we was
in kindergarten. Now, forty years later, we was still good
friends. Last night, I go through our high school yearbook.
How young we look back then! I'm looking forward to your
visit next month. We have a lot to talk about then.

Love,

Shirley

Proofreader's Marks
Add text:
are Loyal friends ^ important.
Change text:
wrote Yesterday, I ~~write~~ to my good friend. ^
See all Proofreader's Marks on page ix.

41 How Do Nouns Work in a Sentence?

They Can Be the Subject or the Object.

- Nouns can be the **subject** of a sentence.

  My **friend** lives in the United States now.
       subject

- Nouns can also be the **object** of an action verb. To find the object, turn the verb into a question such as: "Visit whom?" Your answer is the object.

  My friend's parents visit my **friend** every year.
                             verb   object

- Many English sentences follow this pattern: **subject → verb → object**.

  Marissa has **loyalty** to both countries.
  subject   verb   object

  Sometimes world events influence her **loyalties**.
          subject   verb   object

Try It

A. Read each sentence. Write **subject** if the underlined noun is a subject. Write **object** if it is an object.

1. The country where Marissa was born suffers from poverty. _____

2. Many people do not have enough food to eat. _____

3. Marissa makes donations to charities. _____

4. Her generous donations help many people get food. _____

5. Marissa's loyalty to that country helps many people. _____

B. Write a noun to complete each sentence. Then circle the subjects and underline the objects.

6. My friend feels _____ to the United States, too.

7. Sometimes _____ dislikes the politics.

8. Events happening around the world influence those _____.

C. Answer the questions about world events and loyalties. Circle each subject
and underline each object.

9. What world events affect the world today? _____

    _____

10. How do the events influence people? _____

    _____

11. How do the events change your loyalties? _____

    _____

D. (12–14) Sometimes wars affect people's loyalty. Write at least three sentences
about the Revolutionary War, the Civil War, or another war. Tell how the war might
have affected loyalties. Use a subject and object in each sentence.

_____

_____

_____

_____

_____

Edit It

E. (15–20) Edit the paragraph. Add six missing subjects or objects.

The United States fought a war in Vietnam in the 1960s and
1970s. The United States sent to Vietnam. Some disliked the .
They organized to protest the war. Some marchers carried
expressing their beliefs. The war tested their to the United
States government.

Proofreader's Marks
Add text:
war
A influences loyalties.
^
See all Proofreader's Marks on page ix.

42 Why Are There So Many Pronouns?

Some Work as Subjects, and Some Work as Objects.

- Use a **subject pronoun** as the subject of a sentence.

    My **mom** is running for mayor. **She** will be good for our city.

    Mom is running against **Mr. Greene**. **He** is the mayor now.

- Use an **object pronoun** as the object of the verb.

    The **election** is next month. I will watch **it** closely.

    My loyalties are with **Mom**. I support **her**.

Pronouns	
Subject	Object
I	me
you	you
he	him
she	her
it	it

Try It

A. **Use pronouns from the chart to complete the sentences. Then underline the noun each pronoun stands for.**

1. My mom will be a good mayor. _____ is organized and smart.

2. I respect my mom and her politics. That is why I will vote for _____.

3. The city needs to have a strong mayor. Mom can help _____ grow.

4. "Rosa, please read this. Then _____ might vote for Mom," I advised my friend.

5. Mr. Lopez is helping with Mom's campaign. We appreciate _____ very much.

B. **(6–12) Write pronouns from the chart to complete the paragraph.**

In the last election, Rosa voted for Mr. Greene. _____ supported

_____. Now her loyalty has changed. _____ is with my

mom. Rosa was disappointed with Mr. Greene. _____ did not keep his

promises. "_____ think your mom will help other residents in the city

and _____," Rosa said. "Your mom will make this city a better place to

live. That's why I support _____."

C. Complete the sentences. Use a subject or object pronoun in each one.

13. At school, _____ ran for _____. I supported _____
    because _____
    _____.

14. In our town, _____ ran for _____. I supported _____
    because _____
    _____.

15. In the presidential election, _____ won. _____
    _____.

D. (16–20) Some people have a favorite celebrity. Then their loyalty changes to a different celebrity. Write at least five sentences about a celebrity you used to like and one you like now. Use both subject and object pronouns.

_____

_____

_____

_____

_____

_____

E. (21–25) Edit the news article. Fix five mistakes with pronouns.

Mrs. Sonja Nelson Wins Election

Yesterday, Mrs. Sonja Nelson won the mayoral election. It was a landslide victory. Her received a large majority of the vote. Mr. Roberts was defeated. Him did not receive enough votes. Mrs. Nelson thanked each and every supporter. "Him supported it, and it won," she said.

Proofreader's Marks

Change text:
                                    She
Mrs. Nelson won. H̶e̶ is
our next mayor. ∧

See all Proofreader's Marks on page ix.

43 Do You Ever Talk About Yourself?

Then Learn to Use the Words *I* and *Me*.

Subject Pronoun: I

- Use the pronoun **I** in the subject of a sentence.

  I like baseball.

- In a compound subject, name yourself last.

  Correct: Dad and I go to a game every summer.

  Correct: He and I cheer for the same team.

  Incorrect: Me and dad go to a game every summer.

Object Pronoun: me

- Use the pronoun **me** as the object.

  Dad takes **me** to the game.

- In a compound object, name yourself last.

  Correct: My brother teases **Dad and me** about our loyalty.

  Correct: He teases **him and me**.

  Incorrect: He teases me and him.

Try It

A. Write I or me to complete each sentence.

1. My family and _____ live in Boston.

2. For that reason, _____ am a loyal Boston baseball fan.

3. Sometimes, my friends go to the games with _____.

4. The players always entertain my friends and _____.

5. Will _____ always be loyal to the Boston team?

B. (6–13) Write I or me to complete the paragraph.

Soon _____ will move to New York City. A New York college

accepted _____. Right now, _____ do not like the New York

baseball team. The team angers my friends and _____. My family and

_____ wonder, though. Will _____ change my loyalty? Then

my friends will tease _____. They might call _____ a traitor.

C. Answer the questions. Use **I** or **me** in each answer.

14. What sports team are your friends and you loyal to? _____

_____

15. Have you ever changed your loyalty? _____

_____

16. How does the team entertain your friends and you? _____

_____

D. (17–20) Write at least four sentences to give your opinion about loyalty to sports teams. Use **I** or **me** in each sentence.

_____

_____

_____

_____

_____

Edit It

E. (21–25) Edit the journal entry below. Fix five mistakes with pronouns.

October 15

My brother and I went to the game today. The train picked my brother and I up at the station. It dropped me and my brother off in Boston. Me bought some popcorn. The game pleased I. That's because my team won. My brother and I are loyal fans, though. We like our team whether they win or lose. I and my brother will go to another game soon.

Proofreader's Marks

Change text:

Craig and I.

~~Me and Craig~~ are loyal fans.

See all Proofreader's Marks on page ix.

44 Which Pronouns Refer to More Than One Person?

We, You, They, and Us, You, Them

- Use a **subject pronoun** as the subject.

  My **parents** are from Los Angeles.
  They have lived in Chicago for twenty years.
  subject

  My siblings and I are from Chicago.
  We have always lived here.
  subject

Pronouns	
Subject	**Object**
we	us
you	you
they	them

- Use an **object pronoun** as the object of the verb.

  My parents are loyal to the Los Angeles sports **teams**.
  My parents watch **them** on TV.
  object

  We are loyal to the Chicago teams. Mom and Dad take **us** to see them.
  object

Try It

A. Write pronouns from the chart to complete the sentences. Then underline the noun each pronoun stands for.

1. Mom and Dad are loyal to Los Angeles teams. _____ have not changed their loyalty in twenty years.

2. I try to convince Mom and Dad. I want _____ to change their loyalty.

3. My siblings and I have a plan. _____ get season tickets for our parents.

4. My parents are shocked by my siblings and me. Dad thanks _____.

5. My parents enjoy the games. Mom likes _____ so much that she becomes a fan.

6. After twenty years, my parents finally switch their loyalty. _____ still like Los Angeles, but Chicago is the best!

B. Edit each sentence. Fix the plural pronouns.

Proofreader's Marks

Change text:

We~~us~~ enjoy the game.

See all Proofreader's Marks on page ix.

7. My friends ask we to go to a hockey game.

8. Us have never really liked hockey.

9. We tell they that we are loyal basketball fans.

10. They convince we to go, though.

11. After the game, us thank our friends.

12. Them definitely changed our minds about hockey!

Write It

C. Complete the sentences about sports loyalties. Use at least two plural subject pronouns and two plural object pronouns.

13. My friends like _____. _____

14. My family and I prefer _____. _____
    _____

15. Sports are important. I _____.

16. My schoolmates and I _____. The school takes _____
    _____.

D. (17–20) Write at least four sentences to tell how friends or family members have changed sports loyalties over time. Use a plural pronoun in each sentence.

_____

_____

_____

_____

_____

_____

45 Use Subject and Object Pronouns

Remember: Use a subject pronoun as the subject of a sentence. Use an object pronoun as the object of the verb.

Subject Pronouns	I	you	he	she	it	we	you	they
Object Pronouns	me	you	him	her	it	us	you	them

My friends and **I** love to eat ice cream in the summer. **We** go to the same ice cream stand every year. **It** has the best ice cream. Will **you** join **us** today? Tony and Alex are driving. **We** can ask **them** for a ride. **They** will take **us**.

Try It

A. Rewrite the sentences. Use pronouns for the underlined words.

1. When Tony and Alex get to the ice cream stand, Tony and Alex are surprised. _____

   _____

2. The ice cream stand has new owners. _____

   _____

3. Tony says, "I am surprised, but Alex and I should try the new ice cream." _____

   _____

4. The ice cream doesn't interest Tony and Alex at all. _____

   _____

5. Tony has been a loyal customer for years, but now Tony wants to try a new place. _____

   _____

6. The next day, Alex takes Tony to try different ice cream, and it is delicious. _____

   _____

B. Edit the sentences. Fix the pronouns.

Proofreader's Marks

Change text:
~~Her~~ ^She^ is a loyal customer.

See all Proofreader's Marks on page ix.

7. My friends and me love Bucky's Burgers.

8. Us have been loyal customers for years.

9. Now Harry's Hamburgers is enticing me and my friends to try their burgers.

10. My friends want to try they.

11. Them aren't being loyal to Bucky's Burgers.

12. I know that Bucky's Burgers still has I as a loyal customer, though.

Write It

C. Answer the questions about where you like to eat. Use subject and object pronouns in your answers.

13. What restaurant are you a loyal customer of? I am a loyal customer of _____
_____.

14. What food does the restaurant serve? The restaurant serves _____
_____.

15. Who takes you to eat there? _____

16. Why might you change your loyalty? _____.

D. (17–20) Imagine that you could open your own ice cream stand or burger place. Write at least four sentences to tell how you would attract loyal customers. Use subject and object pronouns.

_____

_____

_____

_____

_____

✓ # Capitalize the Names of Groups

- Capitalize each main word in the name of a specific organization, business, or agency.
  Organization: Korean American Coalition
  Business: D'Andrea Italian Market
  Agency: U.S. Census Bureau

- Do not capitalize **on**, **and**, **for**, **of**, or **the** unless they are the first word in the title.
  Council on Foreign Relations
  U.S. Citizenship and Immigration Services

Try It

A. Use proofreader's marks to correct the capitalization error in each sentence.

1. Michael is a volunteer for the Association On American Indian Affairs.

2. The association helps native tribes gain recognition by the United States government.

3. Members of a recognized tribe can receive services through the Bureau Of Indian Affairs.

4. The Mashpee Wampanoag Tribal council was recently recognized.

5. This was the tribe that befriended the pilgrims when they arrived in 1620.

Proofreader's Marks
Capitalize:
I belong to the cherokee nation.
Do not capitalize:
This Tribe endured the Trail of Tears.
See all Proofreader's Marks on page ix.

B. Answer each question. Be sure to capitalize the names of groups correctly.

6. What cultural organizations does your school have?

_____

7. What clubs or organizations at your school do you belong to?

_____

✓ Use Semicolons Correctly

- Use a **semicolon** to join two complete sentences that are closely related. Do not capitalize the first word after the semicolon unless it's a proper noun.

  Hector is Guatemalan; however, he wasn't born in Guatemala.

  Pedro, his father, came to the United States in 1991; Carmen, his mother, came in 1992.

- Use a semicolon to combine two sentences, or use a connecting word like **however** or **therefore**. Place a **semicolon** before the connecting word and a **comma** after it.

  | **Incorrect:** | Hector was born in 1993, his brother was born in 1995. |
  | **Correct:** | Hector was born in 1993; his brother was born in 1995. |

  | **Incorrect:** | Both boys speak English at school however they speak Spanish at home. |
  | **Correct:** | Both boys speak English at school; **however,** they speak Spanish at home. |

Try It

A. **Edit each sentence. Add a semicolon in the correct place. Add a comma where needed.**

8. Most of the people in Guatemala have some Spanish ancestry however they also have Mayan ancestry.

9. Semana Santa is Guatemala's biggest festival it is a combination of both Catholic and Mayan traditions.

10. Artists prepare elaborate sawdust rugs to line the streets they are trampled on during the procession that follows.

Proofreader's Marks

Add a semicolon:

I am Lithuanian;my best friend is Romanian.

B. **(11–12) Write a short paragraph about a cultural festival or celebration that you have been to or read about. Use at least two semicolons in your paragraph. Use *however* or *therefore* in one of your sentences. Remember to put a comma after the connecting word.**

_____

_____

✓Choose Active or Passive Voice

- A verb is in the **active voice** if the subject of the sentence does, or performs, the action. Most sentences are in the active voice.

   Bill Withers **wrote** "Lean on Me."
   Mick Jagger **has recorded** songs by Bill Withers.

- A verb is in the **passive voice** if the subject receives the action. A verb in the passive voice has a form of the verb **be** and a form of the main verb.

   The song "Use Me" **was written by** Bill Withers.
   "Use Me" **was recorded** recently by the cast of Glee.

- Use **active voice** when you want to emphasize the subject. Use **passive voice** (1) when you want less emphasis on the subject; (2) when you don't know who the doer is; (3) when you don't want to mention the doer or place blame.

   "Lean on Me" **was recorded** by Michael Bolton. (We know the doer.)
   "Down By the River" **was written** long ago. (We don't know the doer.)
   Some songs **are ruined**. (We don't want to name the singer.)

Try It

A. Read each sentence. Decide whether it should be written in the active or passive voice. If it should be in the active voice, rewrite the sentence.

13. The annual Multicultural Festival was held by our school on Friday night.

_____

14. Dances and music from all over the word were performed by the students.

_____

15. A traditional Indian folk dance was performed by Devi and Sahira.

_____

16. Their dance was first performed centuries ago in India.

_____

B. (17–18) Write two sentences about a type of music you like. Use active voice in the first sentence. Use passive voice to tell about music for which you don't know the origin.

✓ Use Subject Pronouns Correctly

- Use a **subject pronoun** to refer back to a noun in the subject of a sentence.
  Ralph is Filipino. **He** speaks English and Filipino.
  noun   pronoun

  Ming is Chinese. **She** speaks English and Mandarin.
  noun   pronoun

- Use subject pronouns to make your writing less repetitive.
  Ralph and Ming are each fluent in two languages. **They** are also learning Spanish.

Subject Pronouns	
Singular	Plural
I	we
you	you
he, she, it	they

Try It

A. Add a subject pronoun to complete each pair of sentences.

19. My friend Nastasiya celebrates her Ukrainian heritage. _____ belongs to a Ukrainian folk dance group.

20. The members of the group perform at various weddings and festivals. _____ dress in colorful costumes.

21. I went to see Nastasiya dance at a banquet. _____ was held at the American Legion Hall.

22. Nastasiya danced with a partner. _____ danced the hopak.

23. The hopak is a fast dance. _____ has been around since the beginning of the sixteenth century.

24. The dance includes many acrobatic jumps. _____ require strong legs and good balance.

46 How Do I Show Possession?

One Way Is to Use a Possessive Noun.

Use a **possessive noun** to show that someone owns, or possesses, something. Add **'s** if the possessive noun names one owner.

My mother left a note for us. My **mother's** note was on the refrigerator.

My brother writes notes on our calendar. My **brother's** notes help us keep up with his schedule.

My older sister is busy, too. My **sister's** schedule is on the bulletin board in the kitchen.

A possessive noun can name more than one owner. Follow these rules:

1. Add only an apostrophe if the plural noun ends in **-s**.

I read my **sisters'** schedules to find them today.

2. Add **'s** if the plural noun does not end in **-s**.

Children's schedules can be very busy!

Try It

A. Rewrite each sentence about a family's communication. Turn the underlined words into a possessive noun.

1. The top priority of my family is keeping in touch. _____

   _____

2. The cell phone number of each family member is posted on the bulletin board. _____

   _____

3. A note from my parents on the counter said they will be home later than usual. _____

   _____

4. Messages from my brother are usually taped to the refrigerator. _____

   _____

B. (5–9) Complete each sentence with the possessive form of the noun in parentheses.

Text messages and e-mail are my _____ (friends) favorite
methods of communication. _____ (Paul) messages are short and
funny. _____ (Olya) messages are longer and full of questions. In
_____ (Oscar) opinion, e-mail is the best way to send messages. I
like getting all my _____ (friends) notes, whether via e-mail or text
message.

Write It

C. Answer the questions about communication. Use possessive nouns in your responses.

10. In what ways does your family communicate with you? _____

11. What are ways your friends communicate with you? _____

D. (12–15) Write at least four more sentences about your communication with
family and friends. Use possessive nouns.

_____

_____

_____

_____

Edit It

E. (16–20) Edit the journal entry. Fix the five mistakes with possessives.

May 15

My uncle's house is right next door. My aunts'
house is far away, beside my grandparents
house. My relative's letters keep us in touch.
My familys distance does not stop us from
communicating. My mothers' wish is that we
stay in close contact.

Proofreader's Marks

Add an apostrophe:

My father̮s note said
he would be back in five
minutes.

Transpose:

My sister s̶ cell phone
is off.

See all Proofreader's Marks
on page ix.

47 What's a Possessive Adjective?

It's an Ownership Word.

- Use a **possessive adjective** to tell who has or owns something. Put the possessive adjective before the **noun**.

  My uncle talks about the past. **His children** love to listen.

  My uncle tells stories about my grandmother. **Her family** was very interesting.

  My uncle and grandmother laugh together. **Their memories** make them smile.

Subject Pronoun	Possessive Adjective
I	my
you	your
he	his
she	her
it	its
we	our
they	their

- Match the possessive adjective to the **noun** or **pronoun** that it goes with.
  1. **Uncle Raul** is talking. **His** brother is laughing.
     noun
  2. **They** listen closely. **Their** eyes are focused on Uncle Raul.
     pronoun

Try It

A. Complete each sentence about a storyteller. Write the correct possessive adjective.

1. My uncle talks about his childhood. We love to hear _____ stories.
   him / his

2. Sarah knows many of the stories. _____ father tells them often.
   She / Her

3. My uncle remembers when my parents got married. _____ wedding was beautiful.
   They / Their

4. My family asks my uncle questions about the past. _____ family history is important to us.
   We / Our

5. I don't want our visit to end. _____ favorite family visits are those I
   I / My
   spend talking, laughing, and listening to stories about my loved ones.

B. (6–11) Complete the sentences about a person who communicates through stories. Use **my**, **his**, **her**, **its**, **our**, and **their**.

I have friends who tell stories. We talk between _____ classes at school. _____ friend Oleg tells stories about everything. To share details about _____ day, he tells a story. _____ details might include where, when, why, or how something happened. His sister Katya also tells stories to describe activities, like a trip to the mall or how she found _____ great new outfit. Oleg and Katya are interesting. _____ stories help me imagine details about their experiences.

Write It

C. Answer the questions about communicating through stories. Use possessive adjectives.

12. Who do you know who likes to communicate through stories? _____

_____

13. How do you use storytelling in your communication with others? _____

_____

14. What types of details do you and your friends or family share through stories? _____

_____

15. How is storytelling different from just sharing facts? _____

_____

16. Why do you think some people tend to tell stories, while others do not? _____

_____

D. (17–20) Write at least four sentences that tell more about storytelling as a way to communicate. Use possessive adjectives.

_____

_____

_____

_____

_____

48 What Are the Possessive Pronouns?

Mine, Yours, His, Hers, Ours, and Theirs

Possessive Adjectives	my	your	her	his	our	their
Possessive Pronouns	mine	yours	hers	his	ours	theirs

Possessive adjectives are used before a **noun**.	**Possessive pronouns** stand alone.
This is **my** photograph.	This photograph is **mine**.
Your song is beautiful.	The song is **yours**.
This photo album is full of **our** pictures.	The pictures are **ours**.
Her letter is sealed with a stamp.	The letter is **hers**.
They sell sculptures at **their** art gallery.	The art gallery is **theirs**.

Try It

A. Write the possessive pronoun that corresponds to the underlined words. Then rewrite each sentence with the possessive pronoun.

1. We wrote this song about friendship. It is <u>our song</u>. _____

   _____

2. This letter is <u>her letter</u>. _____

   _____

3. The letter is from her father. The words are <u>his words</u>. _____

   _____

4. The pictures in the photo album are <u>their pictures</u>. _____

   _____

5. They gave the photo album to me. It is <u>my photo album</u>. _____

   _____

B. Form sentence pairs about creative ways to communicate. Draw a line from the first sentence to the one that contains the correct possessive pronoun.

6. My friend wrote me a letter.   It is hers.

7. I wrote a song to   It is theirs.
   thank my brother.

8. The author wrote a   It is his.
   poem for his daughter.

9. Our art teacher painted a picture   It is mine.
   for us to hang in our class.

10. We gave my grandparents   It is ours.
    a photo album with pictures
    we took throughout the year.

Write It

C. Answer the questions about creative ways of communicating. Use possessive pronouns.

11. What creative forms of communication have you received from family and friends?

    _____

12. What creative means of communication have you used with loved ones? _____

13. What traits make communication through a song or poem special? _____

14. Describe a song, poem, or photograph you received and cherish. Tell about the person
    who gave it to you. _____

15. What have you learned about others through photographs, pictures, songs, or poems
    that you might not have learned through a conversation? _____

D. (16–20) Write at least five additional sentences about creative forms of
communication you have shared with others. Use possessive pronouns.

_____

_____

_____

_____

_____

_____

© National Geographic Learning, a part of Cengage Learning, Inc.

49 What's a Reflexive Pronoun?

It's a Word for the Same Person.

- Use a **reflexive pronoun** to talk about the same person or thing twice in a sentence. Reflexive pronouns end in -**self** or -**selves**.

  I listen to **myself** as I speak.

  My sister repeats **herself**.

  My friends repeat **themselves**.

Reflexive Pronouns	
Singular	**Plural**
myself	ourselves
yourself	yourselves
himself, herself, itself	themselves

- Avoid these common mistakes with reflexive pronouns.

           themselves
  1. People repeat ~~theirselves~~ to be understood.

           himself
  2. Mike says that sometimes he cannot even understand ~~hisself~~.

Try It

A. Complete the sentences with the correct reflexive pronoun.

1. I read my letters to _____ before I send them.
   myself / ourself

2. People sometimes repeat _____ to be clear.
   theirself / themselves

3. My mother repeats _____ to be sure we understand her.
   herself / himself

4. In drama class, we watch _____ act on video.
   ourself / ourselves

B. (5–8) Complete the sentences. Use themselves, ourselves, herself, and himself.

My classmates and I were afraid to speak in front of the class. We surprised _____! We learned how people prepare _____ to speak for an audience. My teacher practices while looking at _____ in the mirror. My mother visualizes _____ speaking to be sure her message is clear.

C. Answer the questions about communicating clearly. Use reflexive pronouns.

9. When might a person practice speaking to himself or herself before speaking to others?

    _____

10. When might people need to repeat themselves to communicate more clearly? _____

    _____

D. (11–15) Write at least five sentences that describe communicating clearly. Use reflexive pronouns.

_____

_____

_____

_____

_____

Edit It

E. (16–20) Edit the paragraph. Fix the five mistakes with reflexive pronouns.

Do people sometimes ask you to repeat yourself? Do you sometimes have trouble expressing youself clearly? Many people have trouble expressing theirselves. I have learned ways to help mineself communicate more clearly. My father repeats himself if people look confused. He says, "When we explain ourself a second time, we should try to use different words to clarify our thoughts." A friend of mine speaks quietly. When she repeats himself more loudly, people usually understand her.

Proofreader's Marks

Change text:

We need to listen to ~~ourself~~ ourselves speak!

See all Proofreader's Marks on page ix.

50 Show Possession

Remember: Use possessive words to show that someone owns
something. A possessive adjective comes before a noun. A possessive
pronoun stands alone.

Possessive Adjectives	my	your	his	her	its	our	your	their
Possessive Pronouns	mine	yours	his	hers		ours	yours	theirs

Try It

A. Complete each sentence about conversations. Write the correct possessive
adjectives and possessive pronouns.

1. My classmates have many conversations. _____ conversations
   <u>Their/Theirs</u>
   reveal opinions and character traits.

2. A conversation can occur between two or more people. _____
   <u>Its/His</u>
   purpose is communicating thoughts and ideas.

3. One boy in class has a habit of speaking but not listening. This habit is
   _____.
   <u>his/hers</u>

4. In class discussions, the teacher reminds us to speak and listen. Our teacher wants
   us to communicate _____ ideas effectively.
   <u>our/ours</u>

B. Complete each sentence. Use a possessive adjective or a possessive pronoun.

5. My siblings do not communicate well. _____ chats become arguments.

6. Sometimes I debate with my friends. I listen closely and respond, based on the
   thoughts of my friends. This technique is _____.

7. My aunt understands people. _____ mind is open to different perspectives.

8. People love to talk to my uncle. _____ sense of humor makes us all laugh.

C. Answer the questions about good conversations. Use possessive adjectives and possessive pronouns.

9. What people do you like having conversations with? I like having conversations with people who are _____.

10. What traits make it appealing to speak with them? _____

_____

11. What actions of good listeners show that they listen? _____

_____

D. (12–15) Write at least four more sentences to describe conversations. Use possessive adjectives and possessive pronouns.

_____

_____

_____

_____

_____

Edit It

E. (16–20) Edit the letter. Fix the five mistakes with possessives.

Dear Mr. Warren,

There is one class I look forward to every day in school. It's yours! In yours class, the students listen closely. Ours eyes are always focused on you. This is because you recognize skills and help us use them to learn. Also, yours lessons are interesting. You bring history to life. You teach us it value in modern society. Thank you for such a great class.

Your student,

Lydia

Proofreader's Marks
Add text: The funniest joke was. ^yours
Delete: Hers stories are the best.
See all Proofreader's Marks on page ix.

51 What Kinds of Things Do Prepositions Show?

Location, Direction, Time, and Origin

Prepositions That Show Location: in, on top of, on, at, over, under, above, below, next to, beside, in front of, in back of, behind

- Use a preposition of **location** to tell where something is.
  On the bus, we talked about our plans.

Prepositions That Show Direction: up, down, through, across, into, to

- Use a preposition of **direction** to tell where something is going.
  We took the bus **to** the movies.

Prepositions That Show Time: after, until, before, during

- Use a preposition of time to tell **when** something happens.
  After the bus ride, we ate lunch.

Preposition That Shows Origin: from

- Use a preposition of **origin** to tell where someone is from.
  We met someone on the bus who is **from** England.

Try It

A. Complete each sentence about communicating at a concert. Use a correct preposition.

1. We went to a concert _____ town.

2. _____ the concert, my friend wanted to borrow my camera.

3. She was right _____ me but had to yell loudly.

4. I was finally able to hear her. I placed my camera _____ her hands.

5. She took several great photographs _____ the concert.

B. Complete each sentence. Write the correct preposition. Then tell whether the preposition shows location, direction, time, or origin.

6. We were in a hurry to get _____ the line.

through / until

7. We were standing _____ a lady with a small number of groceries.

at / behind

8. She is our neighbor. She is _____ Guatemala.

from / before

Write It

C. Answer the questions about challenges in communicating in daily situations. Use prepositions of location, direction, time, and origin.

9. In which locations can people have difficulty hearing or seeing each other? _____

_____

10. What can they do to get their ideas across to each other? _____

D. (11–14) Write at least four more sentences about challenges in communicating in daily situations. Use prepositions of location, direction, time, and origin.

_____

_____

_____

_____

Edit It

E. (15–20) Edit the article. Fix the six mistakes in prepositions.

It is difficult to communicate during a movie. It is quiet enough to talk to the person sitting next of you. But you can't talk too often or too loudly a movie. Other people in front you and in back you can't hear the movie with you talking. It is best to wait the movie is over to discuss it. You can go to a coffee shop during the movie is over and talk about it there.

Proofreader's Marks

Add text:

I put my ticket ^in my pocket.

Change text:

I try not to talk ~~from~~ during a movie. ^

See all Proofreader's Marks on page ix.

52 How Do You Recognize a Prepositional Phrase?

Look for the Preposition.

- A **phrase** is a group of related words. A **prepositional phrase** begins with a preposition and ends with a noun or pronoun. Use prepositional phrases to add information to your sentences.

    We tried to talk **after class**, but we had to hurry.
    noun

    We looked **at our watches** every minute.
    noun

- The **noun** or **pronoun** at the end of a prepositional phrase is called the **object of the preposition**.

Try It

A. Read each sentence about teens communicating. Complete the prepositional phrase with an object.

1. I needed to tell Sara about _____.

2. I saw her in _____ after class.

3. I asked her to meet me after school for directions to _____.

4. We had to hurry because class was going to start in _____.

5. She went toward her class and I went in _____.

6. I wasn't sure Sara understood me until we met after _____.

B. Complete each sentence with a prepositional phrase from the box.

after a few seconds	at a restaurant	on my cell phone

7. My friends planned to meet _____.

8. Paul called me _____ to tell me where to go and when.

9. I heard Paul speaking; however, _____, his voice started to fade.

Write It

C. Answer the questions below about communicating. Use prepositional phrases.

10. What are some situations in school that present problems when people want to communicate? _____

11. What results have you had when you tried to overcome obstacles in communication?

_____

12. What are alternative ways of communicating in these situations? _____

_____

D. (13–15) Write at least three sentences about challenges and problems in communicating with other teens. Use prepositional phrases.

_____

_____

_____

_____

Edit It

E. (16–20) Edit the letter. Fix the five mistakes in prepositional phrases.

Dear Brandon,

 Your sister and I rode the bus together yesterday after class. While I was on the bus, I tried to draw a map your house to mine. The ride was bumpy, so I made messy errors during the map. I ran out of time before your sister had to get off at her stop. I folded the map and gave it for your sister. Did she pass it along of you? If you cannot understand it, please call me below tomorrow so I can explain the directions before you leave.

Your friend,

Mica

Proofreader's Marks
Change text:
It is hard to write ~~at~~ a bus. *on*
See all Proofreader's Marks on page ix.

© National Geographic Learning, a part of Cengage Learning, Inc.

53 Can I Use a Pronoun After a Preposition?

Yes, Use an Object Pronoun.

- Use an **object pronoun** after a **preposition**.

  At the game, friends shout to **us**.

  It is sometimes hard to pay attention to **them**.

Object Pronouns	
Singular	**Plural**
me	us
you	you
him, her, it	them

Try It

A. (1–5) Complete the sentences about communicating during a sporting event. Use the correct object pronoun.

Communicating on the field is easy. I give Cara a signal, and she passes the ball to _____. If she wants me to toss the ball to _____, she nods. Teammates use different signals that show what we need to do for _____. The other team does not know our signals. This makes the signals even more useful to _____. Our coach teaches us about communication. He says every team benefits from _____.

B. Complete the sentences about communication during a volleyball game. Use **me**, **them**, **you**, **us**, and **her**.

6. I communicate with teammates during volleyball games. I whisper to _____.

7. My teammates also communicate with _____ during games.

8. Look for signals. If we point to _____, that means you should spike the ball.

9. Stand in position before Cindy serves. This is a signal for _____ that we are ready.

10. When we play games, our schoolmates yell cheers for _____ from the bleachers.

C. Answer the questions about communicating during sporting events.
Use object pronouns after prepositions.

11. What are ways team members communicate with each other during games? _____

_____

12. Why is it important to have signals that each player understands? _____

_____

13. How can players be sure teammates understood the signals sent to them? _____

_____

D. (14–15) Write at least two more sentences about communicating during
games or events. Use object pronouns after prepositions.

_____

_____

_____

Edit It

E. (16–20) Edit the article. Fix the five mistakes in pronouns after prepositions.

Many signals are used between players during a baseball game. The signals are useful to them. Spectators make signals to they through cheering or booing. On our team, we use many signals. Our coaches make signals for we using hand motions and by mouthing words. People give signals to the pitcher. The catcher makes signs to you that show him how to pitch the ball. The batter can't see the signal. He has to bat without me and has little time to react when the ball races toward he.

Proofreader's Marks

Change text:

The signals are useful to ~~they~~ them

See all Proofreader's Marks on page ix.

54 In a Prepositional Phrase, Where Does the Pronoun Go?

It Goes Last.

- A **prepositional phrase** starts with a preposition and ends with a noun or pronoun. Sometimes, it ends with both. Put the pronoun last.

  Nadja is Farwa's sister. Sometimes communication **between Farwa and her** is confusing.

  Farwa cannot understand what Nadja is trying to say **to her**.

- You can put a prepositional phrase at the start of the sentence to emphasize your idea.

  For the sisters and me, there are many activities to choose from today.

- Avoid these common mistakes in a prepositional phrase:

  1. Use **me,** not **I**:

  me
  Farwa's games are fun for Nadja and I.
  ^

  2. Put **me** last:

  Nadja and me
  Farwa has many activities planned for ~~me and Nadja~~ today.
  ^

Try It

A. (1–7) Complete each sentence about communication between siblings. Choose the correct object pronoun from the choices in parentheses.

Today Nadja is going to the park with her sister. It should be a good day for Nadja

and _____. **(she / her)** Nadja and Farwa invited me to go with them. It will

be exciting for them and _____. **(I / me)** Farwa hoped the games would

be fun for her and _____. **(we / us)** Once Nadja told Farwa that the

games were not fun for _____ **(she / her)** and me. Farwa got upset. She

thought her ideas were boring for Nadja and _____. **(I / me)** I explained

that the games were a lot of fun. I hugged Nadja and _____. **(she / her)**

I am glad we made up. Farwa and Nadja saw their parents calling for

_____ **(they / them)** and me. It was time to go.

B. Complete the sentences by drawing a line to the correct prepositional phrase.

8. Joseph has many friends.
   His little brother Henry
   likes to play

   for them and me.

9. Sometimes Henry and Joseph
   make the rules of a game.
   Henry tells everyone to listen

   to Henry and them.

10. Today they invited me to
    come over with friends.
    I knew it would be fun

    with Joseph and them.

11. Henry said that Joseph was
    ignoring him by talking
    to friends. Joseph talked

    to him and us.

12. We explained to Henry that
    we were happy he came
    along. It was a relief

    to Joseph and him.

Write It

C. Answer the questions about communication. Use prepositional phrases and pronouns.

13. What are common situations in which family members misunderstand each other?

   _____

14. Share an example of a time a family member was hurt due to misunderstanding words
   or signals. _____

15. Share an example of a time that you misunderstood words or signals from a family
   member. _____

16. What are ways to notice when someone has misunderstood, and to explain the truth
   to him or her? _____

D. (17–20) Write at least four sentences that tell more about situations when friends and
   family members miscommunicate. Use prepositional phrases that include pronouns.

   _____

   _____

   _____

   _____

55 Use Pronouns in Prepositional Phrases

Remember: You can use prepositions to add details to your sentences. If you need a pronoun in a prepositional phrase, use an object pronoun.

Sentences with Prepositional Phrases

- Sometimes I confuse new acquaintances when I am **around them**.

- I am very shy. This morning, a girl thought I didn't want to talk **to her**.

- I like meeting girls. But it is hard to be outgoing **with them**.

- My friends and I are shy. It is easier **for them and me** to be outgoing when we are together.

Object Pronouns

Singular	Plural
me	us
you	you
him, her, it	them

Try It

A. Read the conversation between two friends. Add an object pronoun to complete each prepositional phrase.

1. "Paula, I met a new friend named Liliana. I gave a party invitation to _____.

2. But she smiled and walked away. She must not want to spend time with _____."

3. "Kim, Liliana told me that she was happy that you invited her. She asked me if she should bring snacks or games for _____ when she comes."

4. "That's great, Paula. It will be fun for Liliana and _____.

5. Also, you know both Liliana and _____. With you there, we can all probably understand one another better."

B. (6–10) Complete the paragraph about miscommunication with the correct object pronouns from the box.

he	him	I	me	them	they	us	we

I planned to meet Niko and a few other friends at the movies on Saturday. I thought it would be fun for _____ and _____. I looked for _____ in front of the theater at 5 p.m. Niko and I noticed that Victor wasn't there. At first, it worried _____ and me, but we figured Victor decided not to come. After the movie ended, Victor called me to ask where he should park. Victor thought I said to meet at 8 p.m. Luckily, he wasn't angry with Niko and _____.

Write It

C. Answer the questions about a miscommunication that you resolved with friends or relatives. Use prepositional phrases and object pronouns.

11. When have you miscommunicated with a friend or relative? _____

12. How did he or she react to the situation? _____

13. How did you and your friend or relative resolve the miscommunication? _____
_____

14. What did you learn about communicating with others from the situation? _____
_____

15. What will you do differently the next time you are in a similar situation? _____
_____

D. (16–20) Write at least five more sentences about a miscommunication that you resolved with friends or relatives. Use prepositional phrases and object pronouns.

_____
_____
_____
_____
_____

56 When Do You Use an Indefinite Pronoun?

When You Can't Be Specific

- When you are not talking about a specific person or thing, you can use an **indefinite pronoun**.

  Everything is ready for our trip.

- Some indefinite pronouns are always singular, so they need a **singular verb** that ends in **-s**.

  Nothing feel<u>s</u> nicer than visiting family.

Singular Indefinite Pronouns			
another	each	everything	nothing
anybody	either	neither	somebody
anyone	everybody	nobody	someone
anything	everyone	no one	something

Try It

A. Complete each sentence. Choose the correct verb to go with the indefinite pronoun.

1. Nobody _____ that most of my family lives in Argentina.
believe / believes

2. Everyone in my family here _____ English.
understand / understands

3. When someone _____ Spanish, we understand him or her perfectly.
speak / speaks

B. (4–7) Complete each sentence about a student's first day at school. Use someone, everyone, neither, no one, or something.

It is my first day of school. It seems that _____ speaks English

well except me. _____ wants to sit alone in the cafeteria. As I stand in

line, _____ makes me feel better. I hear two girls speaking Mandarin.

_____ of them knows me yet, but I will introduce myself.

C. Answer the questions about learning a language. Use indefinite pronouns.

8. Why might someone enjoy learning a new language? _____

9. Does each person in your family speak the same language or languages? Explain.

_____

10. Can anyone learn a new language? Explain. _____

_____

D. (11–15) Write at least five more sentences about learning languages. Use indefinite pronouns.

_____

_____

_____

_____

_____

Edit It

E. (16–20) Edit the journal entry. Fix the five mistakes in indefinite pronouns or verbs.

November 20

My friend Sasha is from Russia. There,
everyone speaks Russian. feels homesick when
speaks his language on television. Noone
in our class speaks Russian fluently except
Sasha. Each of his friends a few words in
Russian from Sasha. But anybody has the
time to learn more.

Proofreader's Marks

Add text:
Someone
∧talked to me in my
   language!

Change text:
                anybody
I didn't know somebody.
                   ∧

Add a space:
        #
Noone likes to feel left
∧
out.

See all Proofreader's Marks
on page ix.

57 Which Indefinite Pronouns Are Plural?

Both, Few, Many and Several

- Use an **indefinite pronoun** when you are not talking about a specific person or thing.

  Both of my parents know sign language.

  Several of their friends use it as well.

- Some **indefinite pronouns** are always plural, so they need a **plural verb**.

  Many in the world communicate through sign language.

  A **few** of the people we know use international sign language.

Plural Indefinite Pronouns	
both	many
few	several

Try It

A. Complete each sentence about communicating through sign language. Write the correct form of the verb.

1. My parents are deaf. Both of them _____ sign language to
   <u>use / uses</u>
   communicate.

2. Several of their friends _____ sign language, too.
   <u>know / knows</u>

3. Many of my hearing relatives _____ sign language at our house.
   <u>use / uses</u>

4. A few of these people _____ with my parents by writing because
   <u>communicate / communicates</u>
   they do not know sign language.

5. Both of my brothers _____ using sign language at their jobs as
   <u>enjoy / enjoys</u>
   translators.

6. Many of my classmates at school _____ the sign language class.
   <u>take / takes</u>

7. Several of us _____ to use sign language in future jobs.
   <u>hope / hopes</u>

B. Complete the sentences about a sign language class. Use the correct form of the verb in parentheses.

8. A few of our schoolmates _____ sign language to communicate with relatives. **(use)**

9. Several of my friends _____ sign language in special classes. We volunteer at a school for children who are deaf. **(study)**

10. Both of my best friends _____ sign language and use it to communicate with people in various situations. **(know)**

Write It

C. Answer the questions about using sign language. Use plural indefinite pronouns.

11. Have you seen people communicating in sign language? I have seen _____
_____.

12. In what situations have you seen people communicating in sign language? Explain.
_____

13. How is sign language similar to and different from other languages? _____
_____

14. What are reasons that people learn sign language? _____
_____

15. Why is knowing sign language useful for people who hear? _____
_____

D. (16–20) Write at least five sentences that tell more about communication through sign language. Use plural indefinite pronouns.

_____
_____
_____
_____
_____

58 Which Indefinite Pronouns Are Tricky?

The Ones That Can Be Singular or Plural

- The **indefinite pronouns** in the chart can be either singular or plural.

- The prepositional phrase after the pronoun shows whether the sentence talks about one thing or more than one thing. Use the correct **verb**.

Singular or Plural Indefinite Pronouns	
all	none
any	some
most	

Singular: I volunteer at an animal rescue organization. **Most** of the **organization** loves pets.

Plural: **Most** of the **people** have cats.

Singular: **Some** of my **family** loves dogs

Plural: **Some** of my **relatives** love dogs.

Try It

A. Complete the sentences about communicating with animals. Use the correct verb form.

1. We have a pet cat. None of my friends _____ the cat.
   understand / understands

2. All of my family _____ how well I understand my cat.
   know / knows

3. My cat gives me hints. Most of the hints _____ clear to me.
   is / are

4. Some of the world _____ that cats do not have emotions.
   believe / believes

5. All of my cat's emotions _____ easy for me to see and hear.
   is / are

6. My cat is a picky eater. Sometimes none of the food _____ eaten.
   is / are

7. Any of her favorite foods _____ gobbled up right away.
   get / gets

8. None of my cat's behavior _____ me.
   surprise / surprises

B. Choose words from each column to write sentences about owning animals.

All	of my classmates	ask me how to train a dog.
Most	of my family	has pets.
None	of my friends	have a dog.
Some	of our neighborhood	understands how to train dogs.

9. _____

10. _____

11. _____

12. _____

Write It

C. Answer the questions about people and pets. Use singular or plural indefinite pronouns.

13. What percentage of people you know can communicate well with animals? _____
_____

14. Are most pets you have seen trained well? Explain. _____
_____

15. Do most pets you have seen love their owners? Why do you think so? _____
_____

D. (16–20) Write at least five more sentences about understanding animals. Use singular or plural indefinite pronouns.

_____

_____

_____

_____

_____

59 What's an "Antecedent"?

It's the Word a Pronoun Refers To.

- A **pronoun** usually refers back to a noun. This noun is called the **antecedent**.

  Artists paint murals on buildings. **They** communicate through these pictures.
  antecedent   pronoun

- A pronoun must **agree** with its antecedent. This means that the pronoun has to go with the noun it refers to.

  Murals are large paintings. **They** can be seen on inside or outside walls.

  Susanna and I love the mural in the cafeteria. **We** think it communicates school spirit!

Try It

A. Rewrite the sentences. Replace the underlined antecedents with pronouns that agree.

1. In the winter, <u>sculptors</u> carve ice sculptures in the park. _____

_____

2. <u>My family and I</u> go to see the ice sculptures every year. _____

_____

3. <u>Alicia</u> thinks the artist is communicating about daily life through the sculptures. _____

_____

B. (4–7) Complete each sentence with a pronoun from the box. Match it to the antecedent.

| it | he | she | they |

Tonya paints murals for a living. _____ always communicates a message. Parents ask her to paint murals in children's rooms. _____ want to create a fun environment. One man hired her to paint an ad for his company. _____ wanted people to buy his product. A mural is what the artist makes it. _____ can be fun, serious, interesting, or persuasive.

C. Answer the questions about creative forms of communication. Use antecedents and pronouns in your responses.

8. What forms of creative expression do you like to use? Why? _____

_____

9. What forms of creative expression are visible in your school? _____

_____

10. What messages or emotions do you think these forms communicate? _____

_____

D. (11–15) Write at least five sentences that tell more about forms of creative expression. Use pronouns and antecedents.

_____

_____

_____

_____

_____

Edit It

E. (16–20) Edit the article. Fix the five mistakes in pronouns.

Have you seen the murals on the sidewalk? They are a new form of creative expression. A local artist, Juan Moya, began painting them one year ago. They now enjoys attention from hundreds of people each day. It stop to admire his art. His work makes people look at things from a new perspective. We has a meaning all its own. This is his message. They is communicated through objects and people that sit upside-down, sideways, or in mid-air in everyday places. My family and I love these murals. He hope Juan Moya paints more of them.

Proofreader's Marks

Change text:

Tim and I sculpt. ~~They~~ We do it all the time.

See all Proofreader's Marks on page ix.

60 Use the Correct Pronoun

Remember: When you use a pronoun, be sure it fits correctly into the sentence. Also be sure it goes with the noun it refers to.

- Use a **subject pronoun** in the subject of a sentence. Use an **object pronoun** after the verb or after a preposition.

    Marco uses **gestures**. **He** uses **them** to communicate.

    My **parents** say that **eye contact** is important. **They** say **it** helps people understand each other.

- All **pronouns** must agree with the **noun** they refer to. This noun is called the antecedent.
    1. If the noun names a male, use **he** or **him**.
    2. If the noun names a female, use **she** or **her**.
    3. If the noun names one thing, use **it** or **it**.
    4. If the noun names "more than one," use **they** or **them**.

Try It

A. Complete each sentence about gestures and body language. Write the correct verb or pronoun.

1. None of my friends _____ that they use gestures or body language.
   realize / realizes

2. Gina communicates through gestures. She uses _____ without even
   them / they
   knowing it.

3. My friend Jeremy uses body language with his arms. _____ crosses
   He / They
   them when he is angry.

4. Both of my friends _____ eye contact with others when they
   keep / keeps
   are talking.

5. All of my class _____ eye contact with the teacher to show that we
   keep / keeps
   are listening.

B. (6–11) Edit the paragraph. Fix the six mistakes.

> Communication is not only about spoken language. It is also about body language. Almost everyone body language. It hold clues about peoples' feelings. Speakers use body language to show confidence. Most of they makes sure to smile and keep straight posture. Most of our feelings is communicated by words, but some of they are also shown through our actions and expressions.

Proofreader's Marks

Delete:

All of my relatives uses body language.

Change text:

Eva knows me. ~~They~~ She knows my gestures.

See all Proofreader's Marks on page ix.

Write It

C. Answer the questions about using gestures and body language in communication. Use pronouns, antecedents, and the correct verb forms.

12. What types of gestures and body language do you use? _____

_____

13. What gestures communicate positive feelings? _____

_____

14. What gestures or body language communicate negative feelings? _____

_____

15. Why do people use gestures and body language? _____

_____

16. Do you think it is important to pay attention to body language? Why or why not?

_____

D. (17–20) Write at least four more sentences about gesturing and using body language. Use pronouns and the correct verb forms.

_____

_____

_____

_____

_____

✓ Capitalize the Titles of Publications

- Capitalize all main words in the titles of publications, such as books, magazines, newspapers, and articles.

  Book: *Tele-Revolution*

  Magazine: *Wired*

  Newspaper: *USA Today*

  Article: "They've Got Your Number"

- Do not capitalize articles or prepositions, such as **a**, **an**, **the**, **on**, and **of** unless they are the first word in the title.

  Vintage Telephones of the World

  The New York Times

Try It

A. Fix the capitalization error in each sentence. Use proofreader's marks.

1. I'm looking for a book called *the History of the Telephone*.

2. *PC magazine* has an entertaining article on cell phones.

3. The article is called "Aren't Phones For Talking?"

4. Did you read "Capturing The Camera Phone"?

5. It was in this morning's edition of *the chicago Tribune*.

B. Answer each question. Be sure to capitalize titles correctly.

6. What is the name of your local newspaper?

   _____

7. What is the title of your math book?

   _____

8. What is the title of a magazine article you read recently?

   _____

Proofreader's Marks

Capitalize:

Joe reads wireless news.
≡   ≡

Do not capitalize:

Nicole is reading The
Telephone /And Its Several
Inventors.

See all Proofreader's Marks on page ix.

✔ Use Parentheses Correctly

Use parentheses to enclose:

- Explanatory information

    The multimedia phone (the latest version of the cell phone) is a popular item.

- The source of factual information. The period goes *after* the closing parenthesis.

    Forty-two percent of people aged 18 to 24 said it was important to own a cell phone with a camera (comScore Networks).

- The source of a quotation. The end quotation mark goes *before* the source in parentheses.

    "Manufacturers want to sell expensive multimedia phones" (Segan).

Try It

A. (9–12) Edit the report. Fix four errors with parentheses. Use proofreader's marks.

Today's cell phones let you do more than just talk. You can figure out your location, shoot a small documentary, and become an amateur photographer with this device that's small enough to fit in your pocket. Soon you may be able to do even more. "New technologies and concepts are coming at us like seagulls swooping after a dropped potato chip" Maney 8 . Cell phones have begun to take on functions of the PDA and the personal computer. For instance, many phones now allow you to download, store, and play music; others allow you to e-mail documents. (Press 17) These phones also known as smartphones are on the way to becoming "a remote control for your life (Press 15)."

Proofreader's Marks
Add parentheses: The first cell phone weighed two pounds (Press 13).
Add quotation marks: "I forgot my cell phone!" she exclaimed.
Add a period: He found his cell phone.
Delete: It it was in the cafeteria.

✓ Place Modifiers Correctly

Modifiers are words, phrases, or clauses that modify, or describe, other words in a sentence.

- To avoid **misplaced modifiers**, put modifiers as close as possible to the words they describe.

  Unclear: Courtney bought a cell phone at the store **with a camera**.
  misplaced modifier

  Ask yourself: What has a camera? The cell phone or the store?

  Clear: Courtney bought a cell phone **with a camera** at the store.
  modifier

  Now it is clear that the cell phone has a camera.

- To avoid a **dangling modifier**, make sure the modifier has a word or group of words to modify. Dangling modifiers usually come at the beginning of the sentence and often start with a verb ending in **-ing**.

  Unclear: While walking home, her new phone rang.
  dangling modifier

  Ask yourself: Who or what was walking home? The new phone?

  Clear: While Peggy was walking home, her new phone rang.
  modifier

  Now it is clear that Peggy was the one walking home.

Try It

A. Rewrite each sentence. Correct the underlined modifier.

13. Courtney's phone had been stolen **while on a field trip**.

_____

14. While searching, the phone rang.

_____

15. Ringing under an exhibit, she found her phone.

_____

✓ Make Pronouns Agree with Their Antecedents

- A **pronoun** usually refers back to a noun. This noun is called the **antecedent**.

  Where is **my cell phone**? Isn't **it** in your backpack?
  antecedent   pronoun

- A pronoun must agree with its antecedent. It must match the noun it refers to in both gender (male or female) and number (singular or plural).

  Antonio still can't find his cell phone. **He** has looked everywhere.

  Ask **Madeline and Lucy**. **They** were using a cell phone earlier this afternoon.

Try It

A. **(16–18) Complete the story by adding the correct pronouns. Draw an arrow from each pronoun to its antecedent.**

Alexander Graham Bell came up with the idea of the telephone, but _____

was not alone. Elisha Gray was another scientist who worked on _____. Bell

filed a patent for the telephone just hours before Gray did. Gray decided to sue Bell over

the rights to the invention. The two men fought in court for many years. _____

never reached an agreement, though the court named Bell as the inventor.

B. **(19–20) Edit the excerpt from a report. Fix the two mistakes in pronouns. Use proofreader's marks.**

Guglielmo Marconi and Nikola Tesla worked separately on wireless communication. He both claimed to be the inventor of the radio. Marconi developed a working transmitter and receiver, but he used Tesla's research. Marconi patented the invention; however, Tesla claimed she was his. Eventually, the U.S. Patent Office agreed and declared that he was the true inventor.

Proofreader's Marks

Change text:

That phone is broken. It doesn't work.

61 What Are Adjectives?

They Are Describing Words.

- You can describe people, places, or things with **adjectives**. They answer the question: What is it like?

- Use adjectives to describe:

  1. how something looks: **charming, crowded, dusty, empty, elegant, tall**

  2. how something sounds: **chirping, humming, loud, quiet**

  3. how something feels, tastes, or smells: **rough, bumpy, sweet, fragrant**

  4. a person's mood: **anxious, cheery, friendly, frustrated**

- Adjectives help the reader visualize what you are writing about.
  The **crowded** streets are filled with **buzzing** traffic.
  The **dusty** road leads to a **sunny** park.

Try It

A. Complete each sentence with an adjective from the box.

lively	modern	peaceful	simple	sleepy	spicy	towering	vibrant

1. Lukas likes to walk down the streets of the _____ town.

2. Victoria admires the _____ buildings in the city.

3. Lukas prefers the _____ trees that line Main Street.

4. She eats _____ food from the sidewalk vendors.

5. He likes the _____ menu at the corner diner.

6. She goes to street festivals to listen to _____ music.

7. Lukas likes listening to the _____ chirping of the birds in the park.

8. Victoria prefers the _____ energy of the big city.

B. Now think of your own adjectives to help the reader visualize how life is different in a big city and a small town. Write the new sentences on the lines.

9. Lukas gives a wave to everyone he meets on his walk.

_____

10. Victoria takes the subway to visit the museum.

_____

11. The building has exhibits.

_____

12. Lukas meets his friend for lunch in the park.

_____

Write It

C. Answer the questions about the differences between small town and city life. Use adjectives.

13. What do you find in cities? Cities have _____

_____.

14. Describe the sounds or sights of a small town. A small town has _____

_____.

15. What is the biggest difference between a city and a small town? A city has _____

_____ and a small town has _____.

D. (16–20) Write at least five sentences that describe a big city or a small town. Use adjectives in your sentences.

_____

_____

_____

_____

_____

62 Where Do Adjectives Appear in a Sentence?

Usually Before the Noun

- Often the **adjective** comes before the **noun** you are describing.
  Bryan rides his **mountain bike** on the **bumpy path**.
  He speeds along in the **cool breeze**.

- If two adjectives both describe the noun, separate them with a comma (,).
  Dennis prefers to draw **huge, colorful paintings**.
  He stays indoors in his **bright, airy room**.

Try It

A. Add adjectives to complete each sentence about two people with different preferences.

1. Bryan uses _____ weights to build his muscles.

2. Dennis sets out his paints in the _____ sunlight.

3. Most mornings, Bryan completes _____ workouts.

4. Dennis sketches in a _____ studio.

B. Put the words in the right order and write the sentences. Punctuate your sentences correctly.

5. enjoys / Bryan / fruits and vegetables / fresh _____

   _____

6. Dennis / likes / desserts / sweet / to eat _____

7. gear / buys / athletic / Bryan / to wear / to the gym _____

   _____

8. boots / jeans / leather / Dennis / wears / and / blue _____

   _____

9. like / Bryan and Dennis / things / different _____

139

C. You have two friends who have very different interests. What makes them different? Use adjectives to describe them.

10. What activities do your two friends enjoy? _____ likes _____ and _____ likes _____.

11. How are your two friends different? _____
_____

12. Describe one interest that you share with your friends. _____
_____

D. (13–15) Write at least three sentences that compare two of your friends with different interests. Use adjectives correctly.

_____
_____
_____
_____

Edit It

E. (16–20) Edit the letter. Add four adjectives and one comma.

Dear Aunt Helena,

I am riding on the challenging bike path every day. You taught me how to go around the turns. I am preparing for the long difficult race on Saturday. The 5K race is an competition. With so much riding, I have legs. I also eat foods to prepare for the race.

See you soon,

Bryan

Proofreader's Marks

Add text:
Dennis uses colorful paints, too.

Add a comma:
He likes his soft, comfortable chair.

See all Proofreader's Marks on page ix.

63 How Do You Use a Predicate Adjective?

After a Form of the Verb *Be*

- Most of the time, **adjectives** come before **nouns**.
  Juan puts his money in a **safe** place. He has a **cautious** nature.

- But if your verb is a form of **be**, you can put the adjective after
  the verb. The forms of **be** are **am**, **is**, **are**, **was**, and **were**.
  Juan is **careful** with his money. His **spending** is **controlled**.

- If you use two predicate adjectives, join them with **and**, **but**, or **or**.
  Ivan is **outgoing** and **generous**. His **hobbies** are **exciting** but **expensive**.
  He is either **broke** or **busy**.

Try It

A. Complete each sentence with an adjective from the box.

empty	excited	sensible	shocked

1. Ivan is _____ about buying new running shoes.

2. Juan is _____ by the prices at the store.

3. Juan is _____ about spending his money.

4. Ivan's bank account is sometimes _____.

B. Complete each sentence. Use predicate adjectives.

5. At the athletic store, the shoes are _____ but _____.

6. At the discount store, the shoes are _____ or _____.

7. Juan will choose shoes that are _____.

8. Ivan spends his money on shoes that are _____ and _____.

Write It

C. Answer the questions about spending habits. Use predicate adjectives.

9. How do you handle your money? I _____.

10. Do you have a friend who likes to save his or her money? Describe him or her. This friend _____.

11. Describe a friend who spends more than he or she saves. My friend _____.

12. Describe a purchase you made recently. I bought _____.
It is _____.

D. (13–16) Write at least four sentences about spending or saving money. Use predicate adjectives.

_____

_____

_____

_____

_____

Edit It

E. (17–20) Edit the journal entry. Fix the four missing predicate adjectives.

August 17

Today, I went shopping with Ivan. He is careless with his money. He spent a lot on shoes that are. The prices at his store are. Then we went to the discount store. The shoes there are but nice. I guess he likes to spend his money. I like to save it. I am with my money!

Proofreader's Marks

Add text:
This is ^expensive

See all Proofreader's Marks on page ix.

142

© National Geographic Learning, a part of Cengage Learning, Inc.

64 Why Do You Use a Demonstrative Adjective?
To Point Something Out

- A **demonstrative adjective** signals where something is—either near or far.

- Use **this** and **these** for something near to you.

  My Aunt Sharon is buying **this fabric** here.

  These buttons are beautiful.

- Use **that** and **those** for something far from you.

  I will buy **that pattern** over there for sewing.

  She will show me how to make **those shirts** over there in the display.

Demonstrative Adjectives		
	Singular	**Plural**
Near	this	these
Far	that	those

Try It

A. Complete each sentence about a new interest. Use demonstrative adjectives.

1. I like to design clothes. I like _____ fabric here.

2. There are patterns for skirts and dresses on _____ shelf on the other side of the store.

3. The clerk points to _____ fabric on the wall.

4. I look closely at _____ shirts here to study the way the sleeves have been designed.

5. I also want to look at _____ dress in the shop across the street.

6. Aunt Sharon asks what material is used in _____ dress here.

7. I will base my design on _____ patterns over there.

143

B. Complete each sentence about an interest that could become a career. Write the correct demonstrative adjective.

8. I had so much fun. I realized that _____ career is the one for me.

this / these

9. _____ patterns over there are my own unique designs.

These / Those

10. My Aunt Sharon told me to go to _____ store across town.

this / that

11. I can make anything with _____ sewing machine in my room.

this / these

12. I will look into _____ design school on the other side of town.

this / that

13. _____ courses here in the school catalog look interesting.

These / Those

Write It

C. You have a friend with an interest that he or she can develop into a career. Answer the questions about your friend. Use demonstrative adjectives.

14. What is your friend's interest? My friend's interest _____
_____.

15. What school courses will help him or her get more skills? My friend will need to study
_____.

16. Does this career interest you? Why or why not? _____
_____

D. (17–20) Write at least four sentences to tell about an interest that you could turn into a career.

_____
_____
_____
_____
_____

65 Use Adjectives to Elaborate

Remember: Use adjectives to add interesting, lively details to your writing. Adjectives help readers see, hear, touch, smell, and taste.

See	Hear	Touch	Smell	Taste
colorful	loud	crunchy	clean	salty
ripe	metallic	smooth	earthy	sour
shiny	tapping	soft	fresh	sweet

    purple   shiny   tangy   delicious

The plums in the bowl will add a flavor to this recipe.
    ^   ^   ^   ^

Try It

A. Complete each sentence. Add adjectives to elaborate.

1. Ms. Bruno picks _____ vegetables from her garden.

2. She uses the tomatoes to make _____ spaghetti sauce.

3. Ms. Bruno chops the ingredients with a _____ knife.

4. A _____ bread will complete the meal.

B. Complete each sentence. Add an adjective from the category in parentheses. Use adjectives from the chart or your own.

5. Ms. Bruno served me _____ food that made my tongue feel hot. **(taste)**

6. She thinks take-out food is too _____. **(taste)**

7. This crunchy peanut butter gives the sandwiches a _____ texture. **(touch)**

8. Ms. Bruno's fruit salad includes _____ colors. **(see)**

9. Cut lemons give the kitchen a _____ smell. **(smell)**

C. Answer these questions about food. Use adjectives in your answers.

10. What is your favorite homemade food? I like _____ because it tastes

_____.

11. What is your favorite take-out food? _____

12. How does your favorite dessert taste? _____

13. What is your favorite snack food? Why do you like it? _____

_____

D. (14–16) Write at least three sentences about whether you prefer homemade
food or take-out food and why. Use adjectives in your sentences.

_____

_____

_____

_____

Edit It

E. (17–20) Improve the journal entry. Add four adjectives to elaborate.

> September 17
>
> Well, I finally decided to try cooking for
> myself. Today, I made a spicy burrito. I used
> a salsa and two onions from the garden.
> When I bit into the tortilla, I was very
> happy with my homemade meal. Maybe
> tomorrow I'll try another recipe.

Proofreader's Marks

Add text:
    tasty
I like ∧food.

See all Proofreader's Marks
on page ix.

66 Can You Use an Adjective to Make a Comparison?

Yes, But You Have to Change the Adjective.

- Use a **comparative adjective** to compare two people, places, or things.
  Jared's present is **large**, but my present is **larger**.
  The necklace is **more beautiful** than the bracelet.

- There are two ways to turn an adjective into a comparative adjective:

1. If the adjective has one syllable, add **-er**. If it has two syllables and ends in a consonant + **y**, change the **y** to **i** before you add **-er**.	**smart** **small** **pretty** **smarter** **smaller** **prettier**
2. Use **more** before most other two-syllable adjectives. If the adjective has three or more syllables, use **more**.	**anxious** **responsible** **more anxious** **more responsible**

Try It

A. Complete each sentence with a comparative adjective.

1. That present will make Inga happy, but this one will make her _____.

2. This gift is cool, but the other gift is _____.

3. I am excited about her birthday, but Inga is _____ about it.

4. I had a hard time making my decision, and you had a _____ time.

5. We were nervous about choosing a gift, but Jared was even _____.

B. Write the comparative form of the adjective in parentheses.

6. The necklace is _____ than the earrings. **(expensive)**

7. The chain on the gold necklace is _____ than the chain on the silver necklace. **(thick)**

8. This charm is _____ than that charm. **(small)**

9. Your present is _____ than what you gave her last year. **(special)**

10. Inga is _____ about receiving gifts than I am. **(gracious)**

11. Which of these two necklaces looks _____? **(pretty)**

12. The note you wrote in the card is _____ than the note I wrote. **(long)**

Write It

C. **Answer the questions to tell about a time when you bought a gift for a special friend or family member. Use comparative adjectives.**

13. What gift did you buy? I bought a _____.

14. What made your gift special? _____

_____

15. What makes your friend or family member special? _____

_____

16. Was the person happy with your gift? Explain. _____

_____

D. **(17–20) Write at least four sentences to compare two items that you might like to buy for someone special. What makes you choose one item over the other? Use comparative adjectives.**

_____

_____

_____

_____

67 Can an Adjective Compare More Than Two Things?

Yes, But You Have to Use a Different Form.

- A **superlative adjective** compares three or more people, places, or things. To turn an adjective into a superlative adjective:

1. Add **-est** to a one-syllable adjective or to a two-syllable adjective that ends in a consonant + **y**.	It was **the roughest** trail I ever tried to ride. This is **the rockiest** trail in the county.
2. Use **most** before most other two-syllable adjectives. Use **most** before an adjective of three or more syllables.	Only **the most steadfast** bikers try it. It was **the most challenging** trail I ever tried to ride.

- Use **the** before the superlative.
- Never use **more** and **-er** together. Never use **most** and **-est** together.

It was the ~~most~~ roughest trail I ever tried.

Try It

A. Complete each sentence with the correct superlative adjective.

1. I went mountain biking on the _____ trail in the state park.

steep / steepest

2. The first part of the trail was the _____ of all.

more treacherous / most treacherous

3. I was not the _____ person in our group.

slower / slowest

4. My friend Sam was the _____ of all on the straightaways.

faster / fastest

5. Climbing up the hills was the _____ part of the trail ride.

harder / hardest

B. Complete each sentence. Use the correct superlative form of an adjective from the box.

| challenging | cool | dirty | easy | experienced | rocky | thrilling |

6. The group leader was the _____ rider of all the participants.

7. The _____ way down the mountain was on the paved road.

8. The turns were the _____ part of the course.

9. I thought the steep slopes were the _____ of all.

10. After riding through the puddles, our bikes were the _____ in the group.

11. I just missed the _____ part of all when I went off the trail.

12. I think this trail is the _____ trail I have been on.

Write It

C. Answer the questions about an intense athletic activity. Use superlative adjectives.

13. What is the most intense athletic activity? I think _____ is the

_____.

14. What are the greatest physical challenges of this activity? _____

_____

15. What makes this a popular sport or activity? _____

_____

D. (16–20) Write at least five sentences comparing two intense athletic activities. Use superlative adjectives.

_____

_____

_____

_____

_____

68 Which Adjectives Are Irregular?

Good, Bad, Many, Much, and *Little*

- Some adjectives have special forms.

To Describe 1 Thing	good	bad	many / much	few	little
To Compare 2 Things	better	worse	more	fewer	less
To Compare 3 or More Things	best	worst	most	fewest	least

- Use **many** or **few** to describe things you can count. Use **much** or **little** to describe things you can't count. Some words can be either count or noncount, depending on usage.

  How **many** confrontations have you had on the court?

  How **much** confrontation in a game is too much?

Try It

A. Complete each sentence. Write the correct irregular comparative adjective.

1. I told Kyra she is the _____ talented player on the team.
      more / most

2. Kyra felt like the _____ player of all.
      worse / worst

3. Kyra has _____ defensive skills than Michelle.
      more / most

4. She is _____ than Luanne at free throws.
      good / better

B. Write the correct form of **good, bad, many, much, few,** or **little.**

5. Kyra feels _____ about the first set of tryouts.

6. I told her the second tryout would be _____ than the first.

7. She made _____ mistakes than Michelle.

8. She has the _____ offensive skills of all of the athletes.

C. You have a friend who is worried about trying out for a team. Answer the
questions. Use irregular comparative adjectives.

9. What do you say to encourage your friend? I tell him/her that _____.

10. How could your friend improve his/her skills? _____

11. What do you tell your friend if he or she doesn't make the team? _____
_____

12. Why is it good to keep trying? _____
_____

D. (13–16) Write at least four sentences comparing the skills and talents of
three people on a school team. Use irregular comparative adjectives.

_____

_____

_____

_____

_____

Edit It

E. (17–20) Edit the letter. Fix four irregular comparative adjectives.

Dear Kyra,

You are so good at basketball. You really are the player on
the team. You should feel strong, but you seem nervous. I think
you have least confidence than Sarah. You are the talented
player of all. I hope you feel good about making the team than
you did yesterday.

Good luck,

Emily

Proofreader's Marks
Add text: worst She is the player on the team. ∧
Change text: better You are ~~gooder~~ than you think. ∧
See all Proofreader's Marks on page ix.

(69) When Do You Use an Indefinite Adjective?
When You Can't Be Specific

- If you are not sure of the exact number or amount of something, use an **indefinite adjective**.

  I haven't spent **much** time with that group. **Some** people in that group are nice. **Many** people in that group do **a lot of** activities that my parents don't like.

- How do you know which adjective to use?

These adjectives go before a noun you can count, like **friends**:		These adjectives go before a noun you can't count, like **courage**:	
many	**a lot of**	**much**	**a lot of**
a few	**several**	**a little**	**not much**
some	**no**	**some**	**no**

Try It

A. Complete each sentence. Use indefinite adjectives from the chart.

1. I need _____ courage when I talk to my parents about my friends.

2. They like most of my friends, but they think _____ kids are not good for me.

3. They don't want me to spend _____ time with these friends.

B. Write the correct indefinite adjective to complete each sentence.

4. _____ friends do positive and healthy activities.
   <u>Several / A little</u>

5. _____ friends are not good role models.
   <u>A few / Much</u>

6. _____ friends are reckless sometimes.
   <u>Several / Much</u>

7. I know there are _____ reasons to tell my parents the truth about them.
   <u>many / much</u>

C. Answer the questions about a time when you needed to tell your parents the truth. Use indefinite adjectives.

8. What did you need to tell your parents? I told them that I _____.

9. What was difficult about talking to your parents? _____

10. What was a benefit of telling your parents the truth? _____

_____

11. Why is it difficult to tell the truth sometimes? _____

_____

D. (12–15) Write at least four sentences about the benefits and difficulties of telling the truth to your parents. Use indefinite adjectives.

_____

_____

_____

_____

_____

Edit It

E. (16–20) Edit the letter. Fix five indefinite adjectives.

Dear Mom and Dad,

Thanks for spending some time talking about my friendships with me. At first, I agreed with only no points that you made. Now, I understand you want me to have much good friendships. I should not spend several time with people who are not making healthy decisions. We have had a little good conversations this past year. I have many appreciation for your advice.

Love,

Denise

Proofreader's Marks

Change text:
       several
I have ~~much~~ good
friends. ^

See all Proofreader's Marks on page ix.

70 Use Adjectives Correctly

Remember: You can use adjectives to describe or compare people, places, or things.

- How do you know which adjective to use?

To Describe 1 Thing	loud	difficult	good	many/much
To Compare 2 Things	louder	more difficult	better	more
To Compare 3 or More Things	loudest	most difficult	best	most

Try It

A. Complete each sentence with the correct adjective.

1. The recent hurricane was the _____ storm in the town's
   history.
   more damaging/most damaging

2. After the storm, people had _____ doubt that the
   neighborhood would ever be livable again.
   a few/some

3. _____ students wanted to help the people whose homes
   Many/Much
   were damaged.

4. Will the new houses make this a _____ neighborhood than it
   was before?
   best/better

B. (5–8) Complete the paragraph by writing adjectives in the correct form.

The old houses needed improvements. It was _____ work.
Everyone helped out. We made _____ decisions together during
the project. Some people were _____ than others at different
tasks. I liked the sense of teamwork. It was the _____ experience
of my whole life.

Write It

C. Your friends and you volunteer to help build a house for a family in need.
Answer these questions. Use adjectives correctly to describe or compare.

9. What is the most important reason for helping others? I think that _____

_____.

10. How does your work help make life better for the family in need? _____

_____

11. What do you learn from the experience? _____

D. (12–15) Write at least four sentences describing a service project teens can
participate in at home or school. Use adjectives correctly.

_____

_____

_____

_____

Edit It

E. (16–20) Edit the journal entry. Fix the five mistakes with adjectives.

July 20

I had a lot of enthusiasm about this service
project. One family's house was in the bad
condition of all. The work was most hard
than the work I did last summer. There was
only a few time to rest—only a little minutes
each day. But watching the family move into
their new house was the satisfyingest part
of the whole experience for me.

Proofreader's Marks

Change text:

We like doing ~~many~~ a lot of work.

See all Proofreader's Marks on page ix.

71 Why Do You Need Adverbs?

To Tell *How*, *When*, or *Where*

- Use an **adverb** to describe a verb. Adverbs often end in **-ly**.
  In driving school, I learned to drive **carefully** in uncertain conditions. (how)
  I learned to apply the brakes **immediately** if a light turned yellow. (when)
  I also learned to pull **up** the parking brake. (where)

- Use an **adverb** to make an adjective or another adverb stronger.
  I drive **very** carefully.
  　　　　　　another adverb

  I was **extremely** nervous driving in the rain.
  　　　　　　adjective

- Adverbs add details and bring life to your writing.
  When the car skidded, I reacted **calmly**.
  I'm glad I listened **closely** to my driving instructor.

Try It

A. Complete each sentence. Use adverbs to add details.

1. The other cars swerved _____ on the road.

2. I held _____ onto the steering wheel.

3. The car in front of me moved _____ out of the way.

4. I pressed my foot _____ on the brakes.

5. I drove _____ away from the cars in front of us.

6. I stopped _____ to calm down.

7. I understood _____ that I had avoided an accident.

B. Add details to the story. Choose from the adverbs in the box.

| exactly | extremely | lightly | patiently | very |

8. One car slowed down and nearly stopped before it _____ hit another car's bumper.

9. I was _____ frightened as the events unfolded.

10. I acted _____ quickly in that situation.

11. I was happy that I knew _____ what to do.

12. A woman asked _____ if I was okay.

Write It

C. Your friend reacts well during a moment of crisis while driving. Imagine you are with him or her. Answer the questions. Use adverbs to add details.

13. What is the best way to react during a moment of crisis? I think _____

_____.

14. What can you do to help your friend in this situation? I can help by _____

_____.

15. What is an unhelpful way to react during a crisis? _____

16. What do you learn about yourself or your friend after this uncertain situation? _____

_____

D. (17–20) Write at least four sentences to describe a situation in which you reacted well in a moment of crisis or an uncertain situation. What did you learn about yourself?

_____

_____

_____

_____

_____

72 What Happens When You Add *Not* to a Sentence?

You Make the Sentence Negative.

- The word <u>not</u> is an adverb. Add it to a sentence to make it negative.
  If the verb is an **action verb**, change the sentence like this:
  My mom **wants** me to help Mr. Bobera.
  My mom **does** <u>not</u> **want** me to watch television.

- If the verb is a form of **be**, just place <u>not</u> after the verb:
  Mr. Bobera **is** our elderly neighbor. He **is** <u>not</u> very active.

- When you shorten a verb plus <u>not</u>, replace the **o** in <u>not</u> with
  an apostrophe.

  1. Mom **does not** want Mr. Bobera to do heavy lifting.

     Mom **doesn't** want Mr. Bobera to do heavy lifting.

  2. I **can not** let him do the work alone.

     I **can't** let him do the work alone.

Try It

A. Rewrite each sentence to make it negative. Use the adverb **not**.

1. Mr. Bobera is lazy. _____

2. He asks for help. _____

3. At first, I like helping him with his yard and house.

   _____

B. Complete each sentence. Use the adverb **not**.

4. Mr. Bobera _____ boring.

5. He _____ do many things, but he knows a lot.

6. He _____ have a strong voice, but he tells interesting stories.

7. I _____ earn money helping him, but I gained a good friend
   and mentor.

C. Think about things you like and dislike (activities, sports, chores, foods). Answer the questions. Use the adverb **not** in some of your sentences.

8. Name one thing you like and another thing you do not like. I like _____, but I
_____.

9. Is there something you do not like but that you know is good for you? Explain.
_____

10. What have you gained from doing something you initially did not like? _____
_____

D. (11–15) Write at least five sentences comparing one thing you like with one thing you do not like. Use the adverb **not** in some of your sentences.

_____

_____

_____

_____

_____

Edit It

E. (16–20) Edit the journal entry. Fix five of the adverbs.

April 4

I didn't know why Mom asked me to help Mr. Bobera on a Saturday. I think working on Saturdays is fun. At first, I didnot want to go. Then, I saw he can do much on his own. He wanted to pay me, but I did want it. He is now my good friend. He is just a neighbor.

Proofreader's Marks

Add text:
                    not
He is ∧ a boring person.

Change text:
                    can't o
Mr. Bobera ~~can~~ lift
heavy things.∧

See all Proofreader's Marks on page ix.

73 How Do You Make a Sentence Negative?

Use One, and Only One, Negative Word.

- These words are negative words: **no**, **nobody**, **nothing**, **no one**, **not**, **never**, **nowhere**, and **none**.

- Use only one negative word in a sentence.

Incorrect:	No one went nowhere before the test.
Correct:	No one went anywhere before the test.
Incorrect:	After the bell rang, nobody could do nothing more.
Correct:	After the bell rang, nobody could do anything more.
Incorrect:	I didn't have no idea that the test would be so long.
Correct:	I didn't have any idea that the test would be so long.
Correct:	I had no idea that the test would be so long.

Try It

A. (1–6) Edit the journal entry. Use only one negative word in each sentence.

November 15

I studied all weekend. I never worked on anything so much. I didn't want no help preparing for the test. I wasn't focused on my task like nothing else I had ever done. Nobody could make me think about nothing else. I walked into the classroom. I didn't want to be nowhere else. Nothing could not stop me from writing until the bell rang. When I got the results, I couldn't never believe it. I got the highest score!

Proofreader's Marks

Change text:

We didn't have to do ~~nothing~~ anything but study.

Delete:

I can't ~~never~~ believe it.

See all Proofreader's Marks on page ix.

B. Rewrite each sentence. Use only one negative word.

7. I was never not so happy about a test.

   _____

8. Nobody did no better than I did.

   _____

9. I didn't have no idea that I would do so well.

   _____

10. On the weekend after the test, I didn't want to do nothing.

    _____

11. I would not have no more worries.

    _____

12. Never again will I worry about no test that much.

    _____

Write It

C. Have you ever expected to perform poorly and then learned later that you succeeded? Answer the questions. Use only one negative word in each sentence.

13. What made you think you would not perform well? _____

14. What can you do to prepare for a stressful situation or test? _____

15. What could you do to help a friend who is worried about a test or competition? _____

    _____

D. (16–20) Write at least five sentences about something negative that you turned into a positive experience. Use only one negative word in each sentence.

   _____

   _____

   _____

   _____

   _____

74 Can You Use an Adverb to Make a Comparison?

Yes, But You Need to Change the Adverb.

- Adverbs have different forms. Use the form that fits your purpose.

To Describe 1 Action	hard	quickly	well	badly
To Compare 2 Actions	harder	more quickly	better	worse
To Compare 3 or More Actions	hardest	most quickly	best	worst

- How many things are being compared in these sentences?
  I wrote **worse** than my friend did.
  I decided to work **the hardest** of all my friends to excel at writing.

Try It

A. Write the correct adverb to describe the action in each sentence.

1. I checked my drafts _____ than I had the first time.
   more carefully / most carefully

2. I worked _____ than my friends did.
   harder / more hard

3. One teacher helped me the _____ of all.
   more patiently / most patiently

4. Mr. Hingis advised me to plan my writing _____ than I had
   better / best
   been doing.

5. I really wanted to write _____ than I did last year.
   creatively / more creatively

B. Write the correct form of the adverb in parentheses to complete each sentence.

6. I did _____ at grammar than at story ideas. **(badly)**

7. I learned that I did _____ of all at being imaginative. **(well)**

8. Now, I work _____ than I did before. **(carefully)**

9. I am writing _____ after taking Mr. Hingis's class. **(clearly)**

Write It

C. Answer the questions about a friend of yours. Use adverbs that compare.

10. What do you do better than your friend? I _____.

11. What skill or talent does your friend do better than you? My friend is _____

_____.

12. What does it take to be the best at doing something? _____

_____

13. Describe a time when you discovered that hard work pays off. _____

_____

D. (14–16) Write at least three sentences to tell about something you would like to improve about yourself in the next year. Use adverbs that compare.

_____

_____

_____

_____

Edit It

E. (17–20) Edit the journal entry. Fix four adverbs that compare.

September 22

My Goals for the New School Year

English: I work well on short assignments. I need
to do this year than last year on long essays.

Math: I should work carefully on my homework
than I did last year.

Science: I work faster of all in the labs. I clean
up the better of all. I need to improve this.

Proofreader's Marks

Add text:

    most
You helped me of all.
             ^

Change text:
          more
I work most patiently
than I did last year.

See all Proofreader's Marks
on page ix.

75 Use Adverbs Correctly

Remember: You can use adverbs to describe and compare actions.
An adverb can also make another adverb or adjective stronger.

Describe	Compare	Make Stronger
I sat **quietly** waiting for the results.	I reacted **more calmly** than my friend did.	The school election results are **completely** surprising to me.
The students cheered **enthusiastically**.	I think **best** when I am relaxed.	The assembly hall is **very** noisy.

Try It

A. Write adverbs to add details to the sentences.

1. I stood up _____ when the principal said my name.

2. I reacted _____ than the other candidates.

3. The cheers for me were _____ loud.

4. I _____ realized that I was voted class president.

5. I was _____ grateful to all of the people who voted for me.

6. Afterward, a student said I spoke the_____ of all the candidates.

B. Write the correct adverb to complete each sentence.

7. My election team worked _____ than the other team.
   hard / harder

8. I focused _____ intently on the issues than the other candidate.
   more / most

9. The support I got from my classmates made me _____ proud.
   incredible / incredibly

10. I realized that I succeed _____ of all when I really believe in something.
   better / best

Write It

C. Answer these questions about the importance of personal accomplishments. Use adverbs correctly to describe or compare actions.

11. Compare two students you know who compete with each other in a sport or school activity. _____

_____

12. How can being good at something make a big change in your life? _____

_____

13. When have you felt that something you accomplished was going to change your life for the better? _____

_____

D. (14–17) Write at least four sentences describing your friends and comparing their talents, skills, or personalities. Use adverbs in your sentences.

_____

_____

_____

_____

_____

Edit It

E. (18–20) Edit the newsletter. Fix the three mistakes with adverbs.

Haven School Newsletter

The students voted individually in the voting booths last Friday. They careful considered all of the candidates. Out of all of the choices, Annie Broderick more impressed the student body. The teachers are extreme proud of her and the other candidates for their hard work. Congratulations, Annie!

Proofreader's Marks

Change text:

She campaigned ~~better~~ best of all.

See all Proofreader's Marks on page ix.

✔ Capitalize Quotations Correctly

When quoting only part of a sentence, capitalize the first word of the quotation
only if it is:

- a proper noun, such as Amy Tan or China

   As a Chinese American writer, "**Amy Tan** often explores immigration
   themes," such as the conflict between a Chinese-born mother and her
   American-born daughter.

- the first word of a sentence and you are quoting the entire sentence

   Thus, the mother says to Jing-mei in Chinese: "**Only** one kind of daughter
   can live in this house. Obedient daughter!"

This rule also applies to poetry. Whether or not you capitalize the first word, the
rest of the quotation should follow the poet's capitalization.

   The speaker urges readers to guard their "dreams / **For** when dreams go /
   Life is a barren field / **Frozen** with snow."

   The word **dreams** is not capitalized because it is not a proper noun or the
   first word of the sentence.

   The speaker urges readers, "**Hold** fast to dreams / **For** when dreams go /
   Life is a barren field / **Frozen** with snow."

   The word **Hold** is capitalized because it is the first word of the sentence
   and all of the sentence is being quoted.

Try It

A. **Use proofreader's marks to correct the capitalization errors.**

1. Robert Frost is "One of the most widely read and celebrated
   poets in American history."

2. He believed a poem "Begins in delight and ends in wisdom."

3. In his poem "The Road Not Taken," the speaker must make
   a choice, "Two roads diverged in a yellow wood / and sorry I could not travel both."

4. In the end, the speaker admits, "Oh, I kept the first for another day! / yet knowing how
   way leads on to way / I doubted if I should ever come back."

Proofreader's Marks

Capitalize:

   The poem says, "life is a
   barren field."

Do not capitalize:

   Tan says that relationships
   form "The heart of her work."

✓ Use Quotation Marks Correctly

- Put quotation marks around the exact phrase or sentence that you quote from a source.

    Naomi Shihab Nye's poems "**combine** transcendent liveliness and sparkle along with warmth and human insight."

- Do not use quotation marks if you are paraphrasing, or describing what a person said.

    Her poems combine a lively energy with warmth and personal insight.

Try It

A. Edit each sentence. Add or delete quotation marks as necessary.

5. Naomi Shihab Nye is a "poet, essayist, and novelist."

6. The *School Library Journal* said, The author has the ability to perceive and describe her surroundings so skillfully that readers are drawn into these experiences and are enriched in the process.

7. The critic said, Nye gives voice to her experience as an Arab-American through poems about heritage and peace that overflow with a humanitarian spirit.

8. In her poem "Remembered," the speaker says, As if objects could listen / As if earth had a memory, too.

9. The poem describes "how an old man hopes to be remembered."

B. (10–15) Write at least six sentences about your favorite poem or story. Describe the style of writing and what you like about the piece. Include information about the author. Be sure to use quotation marks correctly.

_____

_____

_____

_____

_____

Proofreader's Marks

Add quotation marks:
" I like poetry, she said. "

Delete quotation marks:
She said that she likes poetry.

✓ Check for Parallel Structure

Combining shorter sentences into one longer sentence adds variety to your writing. When combining sentences, be sure that similar elements in your sentences are parallel in form. For instance, if you have two or more ideas in the predicate, make sure they have the same word pattern.

Incorrect: Langston Hughes was a poet, a playwright, and liked jazz music.

Correct: Langston Hughes was **a poet**, **a playwright**, and **a jazz enthusiast**.

Try It

A. Rewrite each sentence so that it has parallel structure.

16. Langston Hughes wrote poetry, created plays, and was enjoying jazz music. _____

_____

17. He was born in Missouri, growing up in Illinois, and eventually settling in Ohio. _____

_____

18. Hughes attended high school in Cleveland, Ohio, where he edited the yearbook, was writing for the school newspaper, and began to author stories and plays. _____

_____

_____

19. In Hughes's earlier poems, he presents dreams that are hopeful and alive, but in his later work, he is writing about a dream that is neglected. _____

_____

_____

20. Hughes evokes dreams so real that people can hold them, nurturing them, and follow them to freedom. _____

_____

✓ Use Adjectives and Adverbs Correctly

- Use a **comparative adjective** to show how two things are alike or different. Add **-er** to one-syllable adjectives or to two-syllable adjectives that end in a consonant + **y**. Then add **than**. Use **more** or **less** with most other two-syllable adjectives and with adjectives of three syllables or more.

    Incorrect: Alejandra's research report is more long than Daniel's.

    Correct: Alejandra's research report is **longer than** Daniel's.

    Incorrect: Lee's reflective essay is interestinger than Renee's.

    Correct: Lee's reflective essay is **more interesting than** Renee's.

- Use an **adverb** to describe a verb or make an adjective or another adverb stronger. Do not use an adjective instead of an adverb. Remember that adverbs often end in **-ly**.

    Incorrect: Claire wrote her research report quick.

    Correct: Claire wrote her research report **quickly**.

Try It

A. Choose the correct form of the adjective or adverb in each sentence.

21. Langston Hughes was an _____ gifted poet and writer.
    amazing / amazingly

22. To me, his poems are _____ than those of any other poet of
    inspiringer / more inspiring
    his generation.

23. The treatment of dreams in Hughes's earlier poetry contrasts _____
    sharp / sharply
    with the treatment of dreams in his later poetry.

24. His poem "The Dream Keeper" is _____ than some of his later
    happier / more happy
    poems about dreams.

25. In one of his later poems, "A Dream Deferred," he presents dreams in a
    _____ light than he did in earlier poems.
    harsher / more harsh

76 **What's a Simple Sentence?**

A Sentence with One Subject and One Predicate

You can express a complete thought with a simple sentence.
In statements, the subject usually comes before the predicate.

Subject	**Predicate**
Teenagers noun	**are** our future leaders. verb
Teachers noun	**mentor** teens and **prepare** them for college. verb verb
Mothers and **fathers** noun noun	**guide** teens. verb
They pronoun	**prepare** them for adulthood. verb

A. Complete each sentence by adding a subject or a predicate.

1. my sister and I _____

_____

2. are an important part of society _____

_____

3. want a lot of responsibility _____

_____

4. responsibility _____

_____

5. grow up to be responsible adults _____

_____

6. every adult in the world _____

_____

B. Form complete sentences. Combine each group of words with a subject or predicate. Circle the complete subject and underline the complete predicate.

7. went to a leadership program in Washington, D.C. _____

_____

8. teens from all around the world. _____

_____

9. our civic responsibilities. _____

_____

_____

10. my favorite activity. _____

_____

11. toured the House of Representatives and the Senate. _____

_____

12. the teens in this program. _____

_____

Write It

C. Use complete sentences to answer the questions.

13. What is one of your responsibilities? _____

14. How does it prepare you for adulthood? _____

15. What adult is a role model for you? _____

16. How does that adult prepare you for adult responsibilities? _____

D. (17–20) Write at least four complete sentences that tell more about responsibilities that prepare teens for adulthood.

_____

_____

_____

_____

_____

77 What's an Infinitive?

To + a Verb

Use **to** plus a **verb** to form an **infinitive**. An infinitive acts like a noun, an adjective, or an adverb.

- **Like all nouns, an infinitive can be the object of an action verb.**

  Mom **decides to go** shopping. What teen **wants to go** shopping?
      verb   infinitive   verb   infinitive

- You can also use an infinitive in the **subject** of a sentence. The **verb** will always be singular.

  To go grocery shopping **is** not fun. **To go** clothes shopping **interests** me.
  infinitive   verb   infinitive   verb

- You can also use an infinitive as an adjective or an adverb.

  I often **have** a desire **to shop**. I **shop to buy** clothes.
  verb   infinitive as an adjective   verb   infinitive as an adverb

Try It

A. Complete each sentence with an infinitive.

1. Many teens want _____ more independent.

2. _____ more independent usually means taking on more responsibility.

3. Some teens want _____ part-time.

4. They try _____ as much money as they can.

B. (5–11) Complete each sentence with an infinitive.

_____ a teen is not all that bad. For example, teens are able _____, but _____ the car insurance is rarely their responsibility. They have the right _____ a job but don't pay a lot of taxes. They eat dinner every night, but _____ it is usually someone else's chore. They have a home _____ in, but _____ the rent is not their worry.

C. Complete each sentence about people in your life who have responsibilities that benefit you. Use an infinitive in each sentence.

12. It's my father's responsibility to _____.

13. It's my mother's responsibility _____.

14. It's my parents' responsibility _____.

15. It's my teachers' responsibility _____.

16. It's my coach's responsibility _____.

D. (17–20) Write at least four sentences about responsibilities that adults have that teens do not have. Use an infinitive in each sentence.

_____

_____

_____

_____

_____

Edit It

E. (21–25) Edit the journal entry. Fix the five mistakes with infinitives.

August 24

I plan to take my driver's test today. Finally, I will be able drive! Once I can drive, I want be more helpful. To helps my mom in every way I can are something I've always done. My mom will help me, too. She will pay for my auto insurance. To buy auto insurance are expensive, and I'm glad that she will pay for that!

Proofreader's Marks

Add text:
                    to
I want drive.
         ∧

Change text:
                        is
To drive a car are
expensive.   ∧

See all Proofreader's Marks on page ix.

78 Can a Verb Act Like a Noun?

Yes, When It Is a Gerund.

Add **-ing** to a **verb** to form a **gerund**. A gerund acts like a noun in a sentence.

- A gerund is often the **object** of an **action verb**.

  I **like shopping** for clothes. I manage some **shopping** every weekend.
      verb   gerund   verb   gerund

- You can also use a gerund as the **object** of a **preposition**.

  The thing **about** **shopping** is that it is a privilege.
               gerund

- Like all nouns, a gerund is often the **subject** of a sentence. The **verb** will always be singular.

  Shopping is not a right. **Earning** money **allows** me to shop.
    gerund   verb   gerund   verb

Try It

A. **Complete each sentence with a gerund using a verb from the box.**

have	rent	set	wish

1. _____ for independence is what teens do best.

2. Jeff thinks _____ his own apartment would be great for Michael.

3. _____ her own curfew is what Rosa longs for.

4. _____ a shorter school day is Jenny's wish.

B. **(5–10) Complete each sentence with a gerund.**

Cole spends his days _____ about _____ his
own car. His parents tell him to start _____. _____ a
car costs money. _____ for a car won't help Cole to get one, but
_____ money will.

C. Teens have to be 18 to vote. Do you wish you could vote? Give your answer in four sentences. In each sentence, use the gerund form of the verb in parentheses.

11. (vote) _____

12. (have) _____

13. (turn) _____

14. (cast my vote) _____

D. (15–19) What rights and privileges do you wish you had? Write at least five sentences about your wishes. Use a gerund in each sentence.

_____

_____

_____

_____

_____

_____

E. (20–25) Edit the letter. Fix the six mistakes in gerunds.

Dear Grandpa,

Being a teenager is so hard! Have to follow other people's rules all the time are awful. Right now, I'm having a problem. I want to drive to the beach. Mom and Dad think that drive that far are dangerous. I'm a good driver, though. I wish I could make my own decisions. Talk to them don't help! Could you talk to them for me? Thanks.

Love,

Sandra

Proofreader's Marks

Change text:

Dealing
~~Deal~~ with parents is hard!

See all Proofreader's Marks on page ix.

79 What Do We Mean by Parallel Structure?

We Mean the Repetition of Patterns in a Sentence or Passage.

Parallel structure makes writing easier to understand.

Use parallel structure in your sentences: Put all the verbs in the same tense, and avoid mixing gerunds and infinitives.

> **To ignore** a school bus's flashing lights is **to invite** tragedy.
> **Stopping** at flashing lights and **waiting** are requirements.
> Be sure to **stop**, **look** both ways, and **proceed** with caution.

To add power to your writing, use parallel structure in your longer passages.

> I will show you that I can be responsible, that I can pass my driver's test, and that I can earn money to buy my own car.

Use parallel structure in lists.

- **Get** more babysitting and yard work jobs.
- **Put** 80% of the money I earn in the bank.
- **Search** online for used cars.

Try It

A. Complete each sentence using parallel structure.

1. I want to get more babysitting jobs, so I am going to ask Mrs. D'Allesandro _____ me to her friends.

2. She knows that I am good at _____ for children, _____ them safe, and getting them to bed on time.

3. I am proud of myself for taking a first aid course and for _____ my certificate.

4. Being responsible and _____ confidence in myself are helping me to find new jobs.

B. Rewrite each sentence to reflect parallel structure.

5. The D'Allesandro kids like watching TV, riding bikes, and to play board games.

_____

_____

6. I plan to save most of my babysitting money, but I plan spending some of it on fun.

_____

_____

7. To save most of my money and putting it in the bank will provide money for a car.

_____

_____

8. I want to buy a used car that runs well, will look okay, and doesn't cost too much.

_____

_____

Write It

C. Follow the directions. Use parallel structure in your answers.

9. Name three skills you have that can help you get an after-school job. Use gerunds.

_____

_____

_____

10. Name three qualities you would like in a used car. Use infinitives.

_____

_____

_____

D. (11–15) Imagine that you want to buy a car of your own. List at least five steps you will take to do it. Be sure to use parallel structure in your list.

_____

_____

_____

_____

80 Vary Your Sentences

Remember: Your sentences are more interesting when you vary your word order and the types of sentences you write.

To vary your sentences, you can:

- Place a **verb** before the **subject**.

  There **are** many respectful **teens**. Rarely **do they cause** problems.

- Expand a sentence with an **infinitive phrase**.

  Many teens try. Many teens try **to behave respectfully**.

  Infinitive phrase

- Use an **infinitive** or a **gerund** as the subject of your sentence. Remember that these subjects always take a **singular verb**.

  To earn respect **requires** good behavior. **Working** hard **is** one way

  Infinitive   gerund

  to earn respect.

Try It

A. Rewrite each sentence. Change the word order, add an infinitive phrase, or use a gerund or an infinitive.

1. I drive carefully. _____

2. I complete my school work to make my parents respect me. _____
   _____

3. I respect other people's rights so that they will respect mine. _____
   _____

4. I can do many things to get people to respect me. _____
   _____

5. Respect helps me. _____

6. Being respectful is an important quality. _____
   _____

B. Edit each sentence. Fix gerunds, infinitives, verbs, or parallel structure.

7. Dressing nicely for work helps me building self-worth and to earn respect.

8. There is times when I come in early or stay late.

9. I always work hard impress my boss, too.

10. Get my boss to like me and to avoid conflict are important.

11. One day I might need get a recommendation.

12. To have a good recommendation are important to me.

Proofreader's Marks
Change text:
There is ways to earn respect. ~~is~~ are
Add text:
One way is behave nicely. to
See all Proofreader's Marks on page ix.

Write It

C. Complete each sentence. Tell what you do to earn respect. Use infinitives, gerunds, or a verb-subject word order.

13. Rarely _____
_____.

14. To _____
_____.

15. I try _____
_____.

D. (16–20) Write at least five sentences about how teens can earn a community's trust and respect. Vary your word order. Use some gerunds and some infinitives.

_____
_____
_____
_____
_____
_____

81 How Are Phrases and Clauses Different?

A Clause Has a Subject and a Predicate.

- A **phrase** is a group of words that function together. One sentence often has several phrases.

  Many **people** / at the restaurant / **believe** / strongly / in smoke-free air.
  noun phrase   adjective phrase   verb   adverb   adverb phrase

  This sentence is complete because it has a **subject** and a **verb**.
  A phrase never has both, so it does not express a complete thought.

- A **clause** contains a **subject** and a **verb**. An independent clause can stand alone as a sentence.

  Nonsmokers want to eat without breathing second-hand smoke.

- **Clauses** that begin with words like **when, because,** and **if** cannot stand alone.

  If **smokers want** to smoke and to eat at the same time

Try It

A. Decide which parts of each sentence are phrases. Write the phrases after the sentence. Separate them with commas.

1. Some people like to smoke their cigarettes in restaurants. _____

   _____

2. Other people want to eat without breathing cigarette smoke. _____

   _____

3. Does one person's right to smoke cigarettes interfere with another person's right not to breathe the smoke? _____

   _____

4. Some states have passed laws to protect a nonsmoker's rights not to breathe second-hand smoke. _____

   _____

B. Rewrite each sentence. Include the phrase in parentheses in the right place in the new sentence.

5. Some people smoke cigarettes. **(at work)** _____

_____

6. Many companies want this problem. **(to figure out a solution)** _____

_____

7. Some companies have separate areas to eat lunch. **(for smokers and nonsmokers)**

_____

_____

8. Other companies have strict policies. **(about smoking in the building)** _____

_____

9. Smokers must go outside. **(to smoke their cigarettes)** _____

_____

Write It

C. What is your opinion on the right to smoke and the misuse of that right?
Answer the questions. Use at least one phrase in each answer.

10. Do you think people should be allowed to smoke in public places? I think _____

_____

11. Do you think people should smoke in restaurants? _____

12. How does smoking affect the rights of nonsmokers? _____

D. (13–15) What is an important right for students in your school? Does anyone
misuse that right? How does the misuse affect other students' rights? Write at
least three complete sentences. Use at least two phrases in each sentence.

_____

_____

_____

_____

82 What's a Compound Sentence?
Two Independent Clauses Joined by *And, But,* or *Or*

The words **and**, **but**, and **or** are conjunctions. They join the two clauses in a **compound sentence**. A comma (**,**) comes before the conjunction.

- Use **and** to join similar ideas.

  The Bill of Rights lists people's rights. It protects people's rights. | **The Bill of Rights lists people's rights, and it protects people's rights.**

- Use **but** to join different ideas.

  All people have the same rights. Some people abuse them. | **All people have the same rights, but some people abuse them.**

- Use **or** to show a choice.

  People can respect those rights. They can abuse them. | **People can respect those rights, or they can abuse them.**

Try It

Proofreader's Marks

Add text:
∧ and
People have rights. They have duties. ∧

Do not capitalize:
A Ⱡawyer can help.

See all Proofreader's Marks on page ix.

A. (1–4) Use **and**, **but**, or **or** to combine each pair of sentences.

People have the right to a speedy trial. The right includes trial by jury. There are witnesses against the suspect. There are witnesses in his favor, too. A suspect has a right to a lawyer. The suspect can waive that right. Would you represent yourself? Would you rather have a lawyer represent you?

B. These compound sentences are missing **and**, **but**, or **or**. Edit the sentences to fix the mistakes.

5. Mr. Newton is suspected of a crime he is in custody.

6. He can defend himself he can hire a lawyer.

7. He wants a lawyer he can't afford one.

8. Suspects have the right to a lawyer the state must find them one.

C. Complete each compound sentence about people's rights.

9. The Bill of Rights lists people's rights, and _____

_____.

10. _____

_____, but sometimes they are innocent.

11. In the United States, are people innocent until proven guilty, or _____

_____.

D. (12–16) The Bill of Rights includes the right to free speech, the freedom of religion, and freedom of the press. Write at least five compound sentences to tell what you think about one or all of these rights. Use **and**, **but**, and **or**.

_____

_____

_____

_____

_____

_____

E. (17–20) Edit the newspaper article. Fix the four mistakes in compound sentences.

Mr. Newton Is Arrested

The police have suspected Mr. John Newton of stealing money, and yesterday he was arrested. Mr. Newton says he is innocent but he can't prove his innocence. Luckily for Mr. Newton, he is considered innocent until proven guilty. Mr. Newton has a right to a lawyer, And he has already hired Attorney Justin Green. Attorney Green will win the case for Mr. Newton, he will lose it. Then Mr. Newton will be declared innocent Mr. Newton will go to jail.

Proofreader's Marks

Add text:
of
The Bill ⌃ Rights has
10 amendments.

Add a comma:
I have rights⌃ and so
do you.

Do not capitalize:
I am glad that we have
R̸ights.

184   © National Geographic Learning, a part of Cengage Learning, Inc.

83 What's a Run-on Sentence?
A Sentence That Goes On and On

- To fix a run-on sentence, break it into shorter sentences or rearrange words to express the same idea.

  Run On: Rosa Parks sat on the bus **and** the bus driver told her to give her seat to a white person **and** she did not.

  Better: Rosa Parks sat on the bus. The bus driver told her to give her seat to a white person, but she refused.

- Avoid connecting too many phrases and clauses with commas. Create shorter, more understandable sentences.

  Run On: Rosa Parks was arrested **and** she was fined **and** she became an inspiration to people all over the country.

  Better: Rosa Parks was arrested and fined. However, her action inspired people all over the country.

Try It

A. Edit these run-on sentences. Break them into shorter sentences.

1. On December 1, 1955, Rosa Parks was arrested and her trial was on December 5 and she was fined for not giving up her seat.

2. On December 4, 1955, people got together and they planned the Montgomery Bus Boycott and they wanted the boycott to last for one day and that day was December 5.

3. People boycotted the buses in Montgomery, Alabama, and the boycott was successful and the people continued to boycott the buses and the boycott lasted for 382 days.

4. The boycott was a protest and it protested the segregation on buses in Montgomery and it led to a Supreme Court ruling and the ruling made segregation on buses illegal.

5. Rosa Parks stood up for her rights and her action led to the boycott and the boycott helped other people stand up for their rights and they all worked together for change.

Proofreader's Marks

Add a comma:

  I learn about Rosa and so do you. ⌄

Delete:

  Rosa did not ~~not~~ get up.

Do not capitalize:

  Rosa was on the ₿us.

Capitalize:

  rosa was on the bus.

See all Proofreader's Marks on page ix.

B. Rewrite each run-on sentence. Break it into shorter sentences and rearrange the words.

6. In the 1880s, Charles Cunningham Boycott lived in Ireland and farmers asked if they could pay him less rent and Boycott said no and no one would work for him and no one would sell goods to him and no one would deliver his letters.

_____

_____

_____

7. Finally, Boycott had to bring in outside workers to harvest his crops and soldiers had to protect them and Boycott's name became a word and by 1897 it was part of the English language and it still is used today and it still has the same meaning.

_____

_____

_____

Write It

C. Complete each sentence to tell about protests. Then reread your sentences to check for and fix run-ons.

8. A boycott is _____.

9. People boycott something to _____

_____.

10. It is important to protest to _____.

D. (11–15) Rosa Parks stood up for her right to sit on the bus. Then people boycotted the buses. What is a cause you would stand up for? What would you do? Write at least five sentences. Then reread your sentences to check for and fix run-ons.

_____

_____

_____

_____

_____

84 What's Another Kind of Compound Sentence?

Two Independent Clauses Joined by a Semicolon or a Conjunctive Adverb.

One way to form a compound sentence is to use a conjunction like **and, but,** or **or**. Here are two more ways to form compound sentences:

- Independent clauses can be joined without a conjunction by simply placing a **semicolon** between the clauses.

  > Oil and coal are limited resources; it's time to switch to renewables.
  > Recycling makes a difference; kids can help.

- You can also connect clauses with a conjunctive adverb such as **however, meanwhile, therefore,** or **thus**. Place a **semicolon** before the conjunctive adverb and a **comma** after it.

  > Earth's resources are being depleted; **consequently,** many young people are working to preserve them.

Some Conjunctive Adverbs
also
consequently
furthermore
however
meanwhile
moreover
nevertheless
otherwise
still
therefore
thus

Try It

A. **Use a semicolon or a conjunctive adverb to combine each pair of sentences.**

1. We need to reduce global warming. The oceans could rise by 7 to 23 inches in this century. _____

_____

2. Some scientists claim that over half Earth's original oil supply has been used. Other scientists disagree. _____

_____

3. Earth's resources are being depleted or polluted. The clock is ticking.

_____

_____

B. Use each clause below in a compound sentence. Write the sentence. Combine the clauses with a conjunctive adverb.

4. Recycling can help preserve resources _____

_____

_____.

5. Students at our school are taking responsibility _____

_____

_____

6. Petroleum reserves get smaller every day _____

_____

_____.

C. (7–9) What responsibility can you take to protect or reserve Earth's resources? Write at least three compound sentences telling what you can do. Combine the clauses with a semicolon or conjunctive adverb.

_____

_____

_____

_____

D. Edit these sentences. Use correct punctuation.

10. Recycling bins are all over nevertheless, some kids ignore them.

11. We want more kids to recycle thus, we put up posters.

12. The posters didn't make a big difference they did help a little.

13. We made announcements; also, we offered rewards.

14. A few kids don't seem to care still, most of us act responsibly.

Proofreader's Marks
Add Punctuation:
The students put up posters⌃ ; meanwhile the teachers ⌃ made announcements.
See all Proofreader's Marks on page ix.

85 Use Compound Sentences

Remember: A compound sentence includes two independent clauses joined by **and**, **but**, or **or**.

- Clauses may be joined by **and, but** or **or**. Use **and** to join like ideas. Use **but** to join different ideas. Use **or** to show a choice.

    Cars use the road, **and** bicycles do, too. You need a license to drive, **but** you don't need a license to ride a bike. Would you rather drive your car, **or** do you want to ride your bike?

- Clauses may also be joined by a semicolon, or with a semicolon, conjunctive adverb, and comma.
    Bikes don't have the right of way on trails; horses do.
    You have to yield to horses; **otherwise,** they might buck.

Try It

A. Use and, or, or however, to turn each pair of sentences into a compound sentence.

1. In my state, pedestrians in crosswalks have the right of way. Cars have to stop.

2. Pedestrians walk facing traffic. However, riders ride in the same direction as traffic.

3. Do bicyclists have to follow the rules of the road? Can they ride against the traffic?

B. Edit these run-on sentences. When possible, use compound sentences.

4. Dad was driving and he didn't stop for a pedestrian in the crosswalk and he got a ticket and he has to pay a fine.

5. Rita rides her bike to work, and sometimes she doesn't ride in the bike lane, and she got a ticket for riding the wrong way on a one-way street.

6. People use the bike path for walking, running, riding bikes, and roller blading, and everyone has to follow the bike-path rules, or no one is safe.

Proofreader's Marks
Add text: *have* Bike riders ⌄ to follow rules.
Add a comma: Rules should be obeyed⌄ and it is our responsibility to follow them.
Delete: Cars have to stop s̶t̶o̶p̶ at crossroads.
Capitalize: please follow the rules. ‗
See all Proofreader's Marks on page ix.

Write It

C. Write compound sentences to answer the questions. Use a conjunction, a conjunctive adverb, or just a semicolon.

7. Why is it important to know the rules of the road? _____

_____

8. What rules of the road do you think are most important? _____

_____

9. What should happen when people don't respect other people's rights to use the road?

_____

D. (10–12) Do you think it is better to walk, drive, or ride a bike to school or work? Write at least three compound sentences to explain your opinion. Then reread your sentences to check for and fix any run-ons.

_____

_____

_____

_____

Edit It

E. (13–15) Edit this journal entry. Fix one run-on sentence. Create two compound sentences.

September 10

Today I was late for work and I was in a rush and I drove too fast and a police officer saw me, stopped me, and gave me a ticket. I broke the rules of the road. I got punished. I'm not happy. I learned my lesson about safe driving. It's important to respect everyone's right to be safe on the road.

Proofreader's Marks

Add text:
                    to
I drove ⌃ work.

Add a comma:
Drivers must drive safely ⌃
or they will be stopped.

Delete:
Rules of the road are
~~are~~ important.

Capitalize:
please follow the rules
= of the road.

86 What's a Complex Sentence?
A Sentence with Two Kinds of Clauses

- A clause has a **subject** and a **verb**. An **independent clause** can stand alone as a sentence.

  Service organizations help people around the world.
  independent clause

- A **dependent clause** also has a subject and a verb, but it cannot stand alone.

  when people need help
  dependent clause

- You can "hook" the dependent clause to an independent clause to form a complete sentence. The new sentence is called a **complex sentence**.

  Service organizations help people around the world **when people need** help.
  independent clause   dependent clause

Try It

A. Draw a line from each independent clause to a dependent clause. There is more than one correct answer.

1. In some countries people cannot grow crops | because they cannot grow their food.

2. There is not enough water | if people there need their help.

3. People do not have enough to eat | if it doesn't rain.

4. Service organizations try to help | when there is a drought.

5. Some organizations have food drives | because they don't want people to suffer.

6. Sometimes volunteers travel to faraway places | because they want to prevent starvation.

B. Write an independent clause to make each dependent clause into a complete sentence.

7. _____ because I want to help people grow food.

8. _____ if their village doesn't have enough food.

9. _____ before I lived in this village.

10. _____ after I got here.

11. _____ when the packages arrive.

12. _____ because I am helping other people survive.

Write It

C. Make each independent clause into a complex sentence. Add a dependent clause.

13. People volunteer in service organizations _____
_____.

14. It is important to volunteer _____
_____.

15. Some people don't have enough to eat _____
_____.

16. I help out _____.

D. (17–20) Do you think having enough food to eat is a basic human right?
Write at least four complex sentences to explain your opinion.

_____

_____

_____

_____

_____

87 Can a Clause Act Like an Adverb?

Yes, and It Often Tells When or Why.

- A **complex sentence** has one independent clause and one dependent clause.

  <u>People work</u> **because they need to earn a living.**
  independent clause   dependent clause

- When the **dependent clause** acts like an adverb, it begins with a **subordinating conjunction**. The conjunction shows how the two clauses are related.

Tells When:	**After** I get out of college, I will get a job.
Tells Why:	I will work **because** I will need to support myself.
Tells What May Happen:	**If** I get a good job, I will be happy.

- **Conjunctions include:** after, because, if, before, when, whenever, while, until, since, unless, although, where

Try It

A. Create a complex sentence. Add a clause that begins with a subordinating conjunction.

1. Everyone should have the right to earn a living _____

   _____

2. _____, people consider my training and experience.

3. They judge me on my experience _____

4. Some programs help people find jobs _____

5. _____, there are jobs waiting for them at the end of the program.

6. _____, people are proud to be supporting themselves.

B. Fix these complex sentences. Add subordinating conjunctions.

7. People have a right to safety they are at work.

8. There were labor laws, many people worked in sweatshops.

9. Conditions were not safe in the sweatshops people were working.

10. The government made laws the working conditions were so unsafe.

11. People formed unions, the unions fought for safer workplaces, too.

12. There aren't as many sweatshops in the United States today, there are still sweatshops in countries around the world.

13. Organizations try to protect workers' rights everyone has the right to safety at work.

Write It

C. Answer each question about the right to work. Use complex sentences.

14. When do you think kids should have the right to work? _____

_____

15. Why do you think kids should have the right to work? _____

_____

16. Do you work? Why or why not? _____

_____

D. (17–20) Do you think it is okay to have sweatshops? Do you think labor laws should protect workers' rights? Write at least four complex sentences to tell what you think about safety in the workplace.

_____

_____

_____

_____

_____

_____

88 Can a Clause Act Like an Adjective?

Yes, and It Often Begins with *Who*, *That*, or *Which*.

- A **complex sentence** has one independent clause and one dependent clause.

  <u>I have school books</u> <u>that help me learn important information.</u>
        independent clause   dependent clause

- Some **dependent clauses** act like adjectives and tell more about nouns. They begin with a **relative pronoun**.
  1. Use **who** to tell about people.   2. Use **that** for things or people.
  3. Use **which** for things.

- Place an **adjective clause** right after the noun it describes.

  Some children **who go to school** don't have school books.

  I am a member of an organization **that gets school supplies for children**.

Try It

A. Write adjective clauses to make complex sentences.

1. There are many people _____.

2. I work for a company _____.

3. I shop at a store _____.

4. Some people _____ collect books and supplies to send.

B. (5–8) Write adjective clauses to make complex sentences to complete the paragraph about a school that has an adopt-a-school program.

My school has an adopt-a-school program. It donates supplies to a school

_____. Many children _____

can't afford to buy supplies. My school asks businesses _____

to donate supplies to the program. My school also asks the students

_____ to recycle school supplies, like backpacks, to donate.

    195

Write It

C. Write complex sentences to tell how the people or things named in parentheses could help provide school books or supplies. Use an adjective clause in each sentence.

9. (service organization) _____

_____

10. (student volunteer) _____

_____

11. (local business or store) _____

_____

D. (12–15) Why is it important for students to have books and supplies? What can you do to help? Write at least four complex sentences with adjective clauses.

_____

_____

_____

_____

Edit It

E. (16–20) Edit the journal entry. Add five relative pronouns.

Proofreader's Marks

Add text:

I know a student *who* needs supplies.

See all Proofreader's Marks on page ix.

June 29

I have a friend who couldn't afford school supplies when she went to elementary school. Now, she is an adult. She has started a program donates supplies to children in need. She works for a store helps her. The person manages the store is a big help. The store has a big bucket shoppers can fill with donated supplies, are sent to relief organizations.

What's a Compound-Complex Sentence?

It's Complicated.

- A **compound-complex sentence** has two or more independent clauses and one or more dependent clauses.

  <u>You have customs</u>, and <u>I have different customs</u> <u>that are important to me.</u>
      independent clause   independent clause   dependent clause

  <u>Because we have rights,</u> <u>I can have my beliefs,</u> and <u>you can have yours.</u>
      dependent clause   independent clause   independent clause

---

Try It

A. Write an independent clause to change each complex sentence into a compound-complex sentence.

The Bill of Rights, which is part of the Constitution, lists some of our

rights, and _____.

People who believe in their customs have that right, but

_____. Freedom of

speech, which is also a right in the Bill of Rights, lets me speak about

my beliefs, but _____.

Rights that protect our freedom are important, and

_____.

B. Write a dependent clause to change each compound sentence into a compound-complex sentence.

People _____ don't have

freedom of speech, but people in this country do. I can say what I believe,

and you can have beliefs _____.

_____, you can have your beliefs, and

I can have mine. _____, our country is

special, and I'm glad to live in it.

C. Write compound-complex sentences to tell about customs that are important to you.

9. One important custom that _____ is _____, and _____
_____.

10. It is important because _____, but _____
_____.

11. When _____, I _____, or _____
_____.

D. (12–15) Write at least four compound-complex sentences to tell about different customs or beliefs that people you know have.

_____

_____

_____

_____

_____

_____

Edit It

E. (16–20) Edit this letter. Make the five corrections to compound-complex sentences.

Dear Aunt Mary,

Today, we read the Bill of Rights, and I learned about some rights are guaranteed in the Constitution. The rights are important they protect us, they give us freedoms. A right guarantees free speech is important. Maybe one day everyone lives anywhere in the world will have equal rights, but I'm not sure that everyone has equal rights today.

Love,

Dan

Proofreader's Marks

Add text:

                    and
You have rights,∧I have
because
rights∧we live in this
country.

See all Proofreader's Marks on page ix.

⑨⓪ Use Complex Sentences

Remember: When you use a variety of sentences, your writing is more interesting.

Expand a simple sentence to a **complex sentence**.

- Add an **adjective clause** to tell more about a noun.
  Use a **relative pronoun** (that, which, who).

  People learn about other countries.

  People **who travel** learn about other countries.

- Add an **adverb clause** to tell more about an action. Use
  a **subordinating conjunction** (after, although, because, if, when).

  They meet people from different parts of the world.

  When people travel, they meet people from different parts of the world.

Try It

A. Create a complex sentence by adding an adjective clause.

1. I am a volunteer in a service organization _____

_____.

2. I travel to villages _____

_____.

3. People _____ don't always have the rights or freedoms

_____.

B. Create a complex sentence by adding an adverb clause.

4. _____, I see how other people live.

5. I like to visit different places _____

_____.

6. _____ , I would change the world

to make it a better place for everyone.

C. Answer the questions with complex sentences. Include adjective and adverb phrases.

7. How can traveling help you learn about human rights around the world? _____
_____

8. Where might you find people with fewer rights or privileges than you have? _____
_____

9. What can you do to help promote human rights around the world? _____
_____

D. (10–11) Where would you like to travel to? Why? Write at least two complex sentences about a trip you would like to take. Use at least one adjective clause and one adverb clause.

_____

_____

_____

_____

E. (12–15) Edit this journal entry. Add two adjective clauses and two adverb clauses to make the paragraph more interesting.

May 29

Today, I visited a village that has hungry people in it. This was a whole new experience for me. I met people. They don't have enough food. This made me feel very sad. I'm going to organize a food and clothing drive. My community can work towards making life easier for people

Proofreader's Marks

Add text:
It is sad to see people. who are hungry

See all Proofreader's Marks on page ix.

Capitalize the Names of Days, Months, and Holidays

- Capitalize the names of days, months, and holidays because they are proper nouns.

  On **Tuesday** evening, the town council held a meeting.

  They decided to extend the curfew to 11:00 P.M. beginning in **June**.

  Unfortunately, it won't happen in time for **Memorial Day**.

- Do not capitalize the seasons of the year because they are common nouns.

  At least we'll have a later curfew for the entire **summer**.

  The curfew will go back to 10:00 P.M. in the **fall**.

Try It

A. (1–8) Fix the eight capitalization errors in the letter. Use proofreader's marks.

Dear Mayor Williams:

I am writing to request that you consider a later curfew on Weekdays during the Summer. Many high school students, myself included, work full-time jobs from monday through friday when school is out. The early weekday curfew means we cannot be scheduled to work the later shift because we won't get home in time. It also means we can't work extra hours on independence day or labor day to earn time-and-a-half. Allowing teenagers to stay out an hour later would give us many more employment opportunities—something that would definitely keep us out of trouble. Please consider this request during the next council meeting.

Sincerely,

Sam Eckman

Proofreader's Marks
Capitalize:
Curfew is 11:00 P.M. on friday and saturday nights.
Do not capitalize:
I don't like to stay out late in the Winter.
See all Proofreader's Marks on page ix.

✔ Use Commas with Introductory Phrases and Clauses

- Place a comma at the end of an introductory clause. An **introductory clause** is a dependent clause that provides background information for the main part of the sentence.

  Because you came home before curfew, you will be rewarded.

- Place a comma at the end of an introductory phrase. An **introductory phrase** also provides background information for the main part of the sentence, but it doesn't have both a subject and a verb.

  After getting home by curfew, I was rewarded.

  The next day, my parents extended my curfew.

Try It

Proofreader's Marks

Add a comma:

By tomorrow evening I will know if I have the job.

A. Edit each sentence. Add a comma where necessary. Use proofreader's marks.

9. If we volunteer at the food pantry we will have to be out past curfew.

10. As a law-abiding citizen I am against that idea.

11. So that we don't break curfew we could always leave ten minutes early.

12. Since we would be volunteers leaving a little early would probably be OK.

B. Complete each sentence by adding an introductory clause or phrase. Be sure to use commas correctly.

13. _____ I tried to make it home before 10:30.

14. _____ I would be in big trouble with my parents.

15. _____ my ride came.

16. _____ I was able to make it home on time.

✔ Use Precise Language

- Substitute a word or phrase with a word or phrase that is more specific.

  Our town has **a curfew**.

  Our town has **a curfew of 10:00 P.M. on weekdays and 11:00 P.M. on weekends**.

- Replace words such as **few**, **many**, and **some** with specific amounts.

  A bunch of teens were caught breaking curfew last year.

  Fifty-six teens were caught breaking curfew last year.

- Add a word or phrase to provide more information about another word.

  Curfews are **wrong**.

  Curfews are **wrong because they are a form of discrimination against young people**.

Try It

A. Rewrite each sentence. Replace the underlined word or phrase with more precise language or add more precise language to describe it.

17. Last night, there was a <u>big event</u> at South Park.

   _____

18. <u>Some</u> kids in town were ticketed for staying out past curfew.

   _____

19. The tickets cost them each <u>a lot of money</u>.

   _____

20. They also had to perform <u>some community service</u>.

   _____

21. The kids' names were printed in the <u>newspaper</u>.

   _____

22. From then on, the kids made sure they were home <u>early</u>.

   _____

✓ Build Effective Sentences

- When joining two sentences with a **subordinating conjunction**, make sure the conjunction goes with the sentence that supports the main sentence.

  Incorrect: If you are breaking the law, you stay out after curfew.

  Correct: If you stay out after curfew, you are breaking the law.

- When combining sentences, keep elements of the new sentence parallel in form. This means they should have the same word pattern.

  Incorrect: I like **going out** with friends and **to work** late.

  Correct: I like **going out** with friends and **working late**.

Subordinating Conjunctions
before, when (to show time)
because, so (to show cause and effect)
although, even though (to show opposition)
if, unless (to show a condition)

Try It

A. Rewrite each sentence. Correct the placement of the subordinating conjunction or make sentence parts parallel in form.

23. Many teens have good reasons for being out after curfew, such as babysitting and to study with friends.

_____

_____

24. Some teens are causing trouble late at night because the curfew applies to all teens.

_____

_____

25. Since it wouldn't reduce crime very much, a curfew would not apply to adults.

_____

_____

91 Why Do Verbs Have So Many Forms?

Because They Change to Show When an Action Happens

The tense of a verb shows when an action happens.

- **Present tense** verbs tell about actions that happen now or on a regular basis.

  My family and I often **visit** Washington, D.C. We **see** the monuments there.

- **Past tense** verbs tell about an action that already happened.
  Add **-ed** to show the past, or use the correct form of an irregular verb.

  We **visited** the Lincoln Memorial yesterday. We **saw** the White House, too.

Present Tense	am, is	are	have, has	go, goes	see, sees
Past Tense	was	were	had	went	saw

- **Future tense** verbs tell about actions that haven't happened yet.

  We **will visit** the Vietnam Veterans Memorial tomorrow. We **will see** all the names.

Try It

A. Describe the visit. Rewrite each sentence, changing the verb to the past tense.

1. The monuments in Washington, D.C., fill me with awe and respect. _____

   _____

2. The Lincoln Memorial impresses me the most. _____

   _____

3. The statue of Lincoln is awesome. _____

4. The memorial has a message of freedom for us all. _____

   _____

B. Complete each sentence. Write the correct tense of the verb in parentheses.

5. Right now we _____ at the Vietnam Veterans Memorial. **(be)**

6. It _____ a black granite wall that shows the names of soldiers. **(be)**

7. The soldiers _____ a long time ago in the Vietnam War. **(die)**

8. Maya Ying Lin _____ the memorial in 1981. **(design)**

9. My mom first _____ the wall in 1982 when it was dedicated. **(see)**

10. Now I _____ before the wall with her. **(stand)**

11. Maybe one day I _____ my own children here. **(bring)**

12. If I do, they probably _____ the same feelings of awe and respect that I have. **(have)**

Write It

C. Complete each sentence about a memorial you have seen or read about. Use the correct verb tense in each sentence.

13. In the past, I _____

_____.

14. Right now, I _____

_____.

15. Someday soon, I _____

_____.

D. (16–20) What places give you a sense of awe and respect? Write at least five sentences. Use the past, present, and future tense at least one time each.

_____

_____

_____

_____

_____

_____

92 What If An Action Happened But You're Not Sure When?

Use the Present Perfect Tense to Tell About It.

- If you know when an action happened in the past, use a **past tense** verb.

    Yesterday, I **dressed** in my best suit.

- If you're not sure when a past action happened, use a verb in the **present perfect tense**.

    I **have dressed** in my best suit before.

- To form the present perfect, use the helping verb **have** or **has** plus the **past participle** of the main verb. For regular verbs, the past participle ends in **-ed**.

Verb	Past Tense	Past Participle
celebrate	celebrated	celebrated
shop	shopped	shopped
try	tried	tried

Try It

A. Complete each sentence. Write the correct tense of the verb.

1. Yesterday, I _____ for a job.
    interviewed / have interviewed

2. I _____ to get a job many times this month.
    tried / have tried

3. I really _____ to get this particular job yesterday.
    wanted / have wanted

4. That's why yesterday I _____ in my best suit.
    dressed / have dressed

5. My dad says that dressing well _____ him find a good job.
    helped / has helped

B. Complete each sentence. Write the past or present perfect tense of the verb in parentheses.

6. Last weekend, I _____ for a fancy new dress. **(shop)**

7. I _____ wearing fancy dresses so far. **(hate)**

8. Now, I _____ to buy something really nice. **(want)**

9. Yesterday, my parents and I _____ to my grandparents' house. **(travel)**

10. We _____ to surprise my grandparents. **(plan)**

11. In the evening, we _____ their 50th wedding anniversary. **(celebrate)**

12. I _____ my grandparents since I was very young. **(respect)**

13. For the party, I _____ in my fancy new dress to show that respect. **(dress)**

Write It

C. Answer each question about how you dress. Use the present perfect tense.

14. Recently, what have you changed about what you wear? _____

_____

15. What kind of clothes have you most liked to wear? _____

_____

16. Have you always dressed the same for school as you have for special occasions? Why or why not? _____

_____

D. (17–20) When have you dressed up to show respect? Write at least four sentences. Use the present perfect tense.

_____

_____

_____

_____

_____

93 What If a Past Action Is Still Going On?

Then Use the Present Perfect Tense.

- Use the **present perfect tense** to show that an action began in the past and may still be happening.

  My family **has recycled** for years. (We are still recycling.)

  We **have tried** to respect the environment. (We are still trying to respect it.)

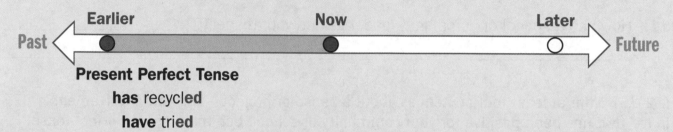

- A verb in the present perfect tense uses the helping verb **have** or **has** plus the **past participle** of the main verb. For regular verbs, the past participle ends in **-ed**.

Try It

A. Complete each sentence. Write the present perfect form of the verb in parentheses.

1. I _____ our mayor for a long time. **(admire)**

2. She _____ important causes in our city. **(support)**

3. Recently, the mayor _____ a recycling project. **(start)**

4. We _____ a decrease in garbage since the project began. **(experience)**

B. (5–8) Complete each sentence with a verb in the present perfect. Choose from the verbs in the box.

endorse	plant	work	vote

The mayor _____ hard to make our city better. She _____ my school's Beautify the City project. As a result, the students at my school _____ flowers in city parks. My parents _____ for the mayor in the past, and they will again.

C. Answer the questions about your community. Use the present perfect tense.

9. How have you helped make your community a better place to live? I _____

_____

10. What are some causes that you have supported? _____

_____

11. How has a school or community leader gained your respect? _____

_____

D. (12–15) Write at least four sentences about a cause or project—and your involvement in it—that has been positive for your community or school. Use the present perfect tense.

_____

_____

_____

_____

_____

Edit It

E. (16–20) Edit the news story. Fix the five mistakes with present perfect verbs.

Mayor Jones Makes the Grade

Mayor Kristen Jones has gained the respect of the whole community. For years, she have worked tirelessly to make this city a better place to live. Mayor Jones has help beautify the city with her monthly clean-up day. People has pitch in to help pick up garbage from neighborhood streets. They has worked together. We are lucky to have people like Mayor Jones running our city. These amazing people have inspire us all.

Proofreader's Marks
Add text: has Mrs. Jones decided to run for mayor again.
Change text: has asked She ~~have ask~~ for our help.
See all Proofreader's Marks on page ix.

94 Do All Past Participles End in *-ed*?

No, Irregular Verbs have Special Forms.

- Past participles of irregular verbs have a completely new spelling.

	Verb	Past Tense	Past Participle
Forms of *Be*	am, is	was	been
	are	were	been
	give	gave	given
	go	went	gone
	see	saw	seen

- Use **has** or **have** plus the past participle to form the **present perfect tense**.
  My family **has been** to Russia. We **have seen** where my dad grew up.

Try It

A. Complete each sentence. Write the present perfect form of the verb in parentheses.

1. I _____ to Russia several times. **(go)**

2. My brothers and sisters _____ there, too. **(be)**

3. Each time, our relatives there _____ us a tour. **(give)**

4. We _____ what life in Russia was like for Grandma. **(see)**

B. Rewrite each sentence in the present perfect tense.

5. Grandma saw a lot of hard times. _____

6. She gave up many things. _____

7. We were lucky as a result. _____

C. Answer the questions about visiting relatives. Use the present perfect tense.

8. What relative have you visited recently? I _____.

9. What has the relative done that you will never have to do? _____

_____

10. What have you learned about the relative that made you respectful? _____

_____

11. What have you given to your relative in return? _____

_____

D. (12–15) Write at least four sentences about how your parents or grandparents have changed your life to make it better than theirs was. Use the present perfect tense.

_____

_____

_____

_____

Edit It

E. (16–20) Edit this letter. Fix the five mistakes with present perfect verbs.

Dear Uncle Toni,

   We are having a great trip. So far, we gone up the mountain road three times to visit the village where Grandma lived. Best of all, we seen the house she grew up in. The man who lives there now have been very kind to us. He give us an open invitation to come back anytime.

   I can't wait to show you my photos. It have been the trip of a lifetime!

Love,

Carlos

Proofreader's Marks

Add text:
   have
I seen the village.
  ^

Change text: has This trip have given me more respect for Grandma.
See all Proofreader's Marks on page ix.

95 Verbs in the Present Perfect Tense

Remember: Use **have** or **has** plus the past participle of a verb to form the present perfect tense.

- The past participle of a **regular verb** ends in **-ed**.
  Dad **has trained** to run in the marathon. **(train + -ed)**
  We **have realized** that he will finish no matter what. **(realize [– e] + -ed)**
- The past participle of an **irregular verb** has a completely new spelling.

Verb	Past Participle	Verb	Past Participle
be	been	see	seen
come	come	show	shown
get	got or gotten	take	taken

Try It

A. Complete each sentence. Write the present perfect tense of the verb in parentheses.

1. My dad _____ a lot of courage. **(show)**

2. He _____ many surgeries. **(survive)**

3. We _____ him get stronger each time. **(see)**

4. Marathons always _____ a hobby of his. **(be)**

5. That's why he _____ to participate in this marathon. **(decide)**

B. Rewrite each sentence in the present perfect tense.

6. We come to see Dad race. _____

7. He races in his wheelchair. _____

8. It takes him a long time to finish. _____

C. Complete each sentence about how Dad and his family have felt after each race. Use the present perfect tense.

9. My dad _____

_____.

10. I _____

_____.

11. My whole family _____

_____.

D. (12–15) Think of a person you have respected. Why have you respect that person? Write at least four sentences. Use the present perfect tense.

_____

_____

_____

_____

_____

E. (16–20) Edit this journal entry. Fix the five mistakes in present perfect verb forms.

June 23

Dad has completed his first marathon in a wheelchair. He has showed us all how to be courageous. I seen Dad bounce back after every surgery. He has hold his head up high. My respect for him have grown every year. I has decide to be more like him in the future. I'm so glad to have Dad for my dad.

Proofreader's Marks
Add text:
have
I seen him race.
^
Change text:
has
Dad ~~have~~ faced many
^
challenges.
See all Proofreader's Marks on page ix.

96 How Do You Show Which Past Action Happened First?

Use the Past Perfect Tense.

- Use the **past tense** of a verb to tell about an action that was completed in the past.

    My older brother **played** tennis with me.

- If you want to show that one past action happened before another, use the **past perfect tense** for the action that happened first.

    He **had won** two tennis tournaments by the time he **graduated** from high school.

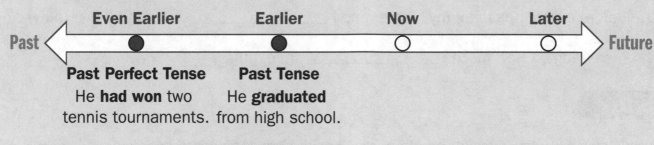

Even Earlier   **Earlier**   **Now**   **Later**

Past ← → Future

Past Perfect Tense   **Past Tense**
He **had won** two   He **graduated**
tennis tournaments.   from high school.

- To form the **past perfect tense**, use **had** plus the **past participle** of the main verb.

    I **missed** him after he **had been** at college for a while.

Try It

A. Complete each sentence with the past perfect form of the verb in parentheses.

1. On the day my brother left for college, I realized I _____ him for granted. **(take)**

2. I never _____ the only child at home before. **(be)**

3. Sure, he _____ me, but now I missed that. **(tease)**

4. I even liked that we _____ a bedroom. **(share)**

5. I remembered how he _____ tennis with me. **(play)**

6. I thought about how he _____ me guitar lessons. **(give)**

7. Now he was gone, and everything _____. **(change)**

B. Complete each sentence. Write the past tense or past perfect tense of the verb in parentheses.

8. My brother had been away for two months when he _____ home for a visit. **(come)**

9. I already _____ to school on the day he arrived. **(go)**

10. When I _____ home, he had already been home for several hours. **(get)**

11. I was really happy that he _____ to visit. **(decide)**

12. My parents and I _____ a big dinner before he arrived. **(plan)**

13. Before an hour passed, my brother and I _____ a set of tennis. **(play)**

14. I realized just how much I _____ him. **(miss)**

Write It

C. Complete each sentence about something else the two siblings did together before the older brother went back to school. Use past and past perfect tense verbs.

15. Before he _____, my brother and I _____
_____.

16. I _____ until he _____
_____.

17. After he _____, I _____
_____.

D. (18–20) Write at least three sentences about a relationship that you have with a family member. Tell about something you did together in the past. Use the past perfect tense in each sentence.

_____

_____

_____

_____

_____

97 How Do You Know Which Tense to Use?

Think About When the Action Happened.

- When you tell about the past, you may need to relate actions in time. First use the past tense to tell what happened.

    Maura **moved** in September.

- Then use the **past perfect tense** to tell what happened before Maura moved.

    Maura **moved** to Glendale, but she **had lived** in Springfield for many years.

- Sometimes a past action may still be going on. That's when you use the **present perfect tense**.

    Maura **has kept** the same friends for years.

    She **has stayed** in touch with her friends since she **moved**.

Try It

A. Complete each sentence. Write the correct tense of the verb.

1. Maura _____ in Glendale since September.
    <u>lived / has lived</u>

2. She _____ up in Springfield.
    <u>grew / has grown</u>

3. By the time she moved, Maura _____ field hockey for two seasons.
    <u>has played / had played</u>

4. She _____ out for Glendale High School field hockey team.
    <u>tried / has tried</u>

B. Complete each sentence. Write the past, present perfect, or past perfect tense of the verb in parentheses.

5. By the time the season ended, Maura _____ many new friends. **(make)**

6. She still _____ her old friends, though. **(miss)**

7. That's why she _____ in touch with them before her birthday party. **(get)**

8. Last week, Maura _____ her old friends and her new friends to her party. **(invite)**

C. Complete each sentence about a friend. Use the correct tense of verbs to show past actions.

9. Last week, my friend and I _____
_____ .

10. Before we did that, we _____
_____ .

11. Since then, we _____
_____ .

D. (12–15) Have you heard the expression "Make new friends, but keep the old"? Write at least four sentences about how it has related to you. Use the past tense, the present perfect tense, and the past perfect tense at least one time each.

_____

_____

_____

_____

E. (16–20) Edit this letter. Fix the five mistakes in verb tenses.

Dear Isabella,

I'm so glad that you came to my party last week. I'm sorry that by the time you got here, we ate most of the cake. Well, at least we have gotten to visit with each other, and that's what counts. I am learning how important it is to have good friends. My new friends here be very nice to me. They will never replace you, though. I has known you for fifteen years! I have learn that good friends are the best gift of all.

Love,

Maura

Proofreader's Marks

Change text:

Maura ~~write~~ wrote to her friend last night.

See all Proofreader's Marks on page ix.

98 When Do You Use the Future Perfect Tense?

When You Want to Relate a Future Action to a Future Time

- Sometimes an action that hasn't yet happened depends on another future event. That's when you use the **future perfect tense**.

    Soon **we will leave on our trip.** By then, I **will have made** all my plans.

    Before we go, I **will have finished** all of my work.

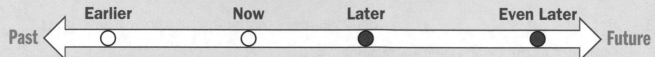

| Earlier | Now | Later | Even Later |

Past ←――――――――――――――――――――――――――――――→ Future

Future Perfect Tense
I **will have called**
Grandma and Grandpa, too.

- To form the **future perfect tense**, use **will have** plus the **past participle** of the main verb.

    Before we arrive at the ferry, we **will have driven** for five hours.

    Before we arrive on the island, we **will have been** on the ferry for two hours.

Try It

A. Complete each sentence. Write the future perfect tense of the verb in parentheses.

1. Just think: By this time tomorrow, my family and I _____ the ferry. **(board)**

2. The ferry _____ us all the way to the island. **(take)**

3. It _____ in the harbor. **(dock)**

4. Grandpa _____ to meet us at the boat. **(come)**

5. We _____ lunch at the fish stand. **(eat)**

6. We _____ at the market. **(shop)**

7. We _____ for fresh bread at the bakery. **(stop)**

8. By this time tomorrow, we _____ at our final destination, Grandma's cottage. **(arrive)**

B. Complete each sentence with a future perfect tense verb.

9. When this summer ends, Lisa _____ ten summers on the island.

10. Right now, Lisa is 16. By the time she goes home, she _____ 17.

11. She _____ her birthday at a place she loves and with people she loves, too.

12. Before Lisa leaves the island, she _____ her boat in the bay.

13. She _____ volleyball every morning, and she will have gone swimming at the beach every afternoon.

14. She also _____ money working at her summer job.

Write It

C. Suppose Lisa will spend one day hiking on a nature trail on the island. Complete the sentences about what she will do or see. Use the future perfect tense.

15. By the end of the day, Lisa _____
_____.

16. When she gets to the end of the trail, she _____
_____.

17. Soon, the sun _____
_____.

D. (18–20) What is your favorite place? What do you do there? Write at least three sentences about the place. Use the future perfect tense.

_____

_____

_____

_____

_____

99 How Are the Past Perfect and Future Perfect Tenses Alike?

They Both Show How One Action Happens Before Another.

- Use the **past perfect tense** to help your readers know that an action happened even earlier than another past action.

     By the time school got out, I **had visited** Grandma ten times.

- Use the **future perfect tense** to help your readers know that an action will happen before some other time in the future.

     By the time my vacation ends, I **will have visited** Grandma three more times.

Try It

A. Complete each sentence. Write the past perfect or future perfect tense of the verb in parentheses.

1. I remember that last weekend. When we got to Grandma's house, we could tell from the delicious smell that she _____ a huge dinner for us. **(prepare)**

2. By the time the adults were finished with the main meal, my brothers, sisters, cousins, and I _____ outside to play. **(run)**

3. After a while, we were called inside for dessert. Even though we _____ our plates with chicken and potatoes, we still had room for apple pie. **(fill)**

4. By the time I see Grandma again, she _____ into her new life in the assisted living facility. **(settle)**

B. Complete each sentence with a past perfect or a future perfect tense verb.

5. Last fall, Grandma got very sick. I thought about how she _____ our whole family together over the years.

6. I realized now how lucky I _____ to have her for my grandma.

7. Before she becomes too sick, I _____ Grandma how much I love her.

8. Before she dies, I hope that I _____ something special for her.

C. Complete each sentence about a family member you love and respect. Use the past perfect or future perfect tense.

9. Before I was a teenager, I _____

_____.

10. Before my _____, we always _____

_____.

11. Before this year is over, _____ and I _____

_____.

D. (12–15) Write at least four sentences about how parents and grandparents keep families together. Use the past perfect or future perfect tense in each sentence.

_____

_____

_____

_____

_____

Edit It

E. (16–20) Edit this letter. Fix the five mistakes in past perfect or future perfect verbs.

Dear Grandma,

By the time you get this letter, I have performed in my piano recital. This morning, I thought about how we used to play our duets. Remembering that made me sad because I know you won't be at my recital. Mom suggested I tape the recital, but I decided to do that already. Before you see me again, you heard me on the tape. You have imagined you were there! By then you will the chance to say whether I was good or bad! Then we can listen together during my next visit.

Love,

Zac

Proofreader's Marks

Add text:
                have
I ̬given Grandma a tape.

See all Proofreader's Marks on page ix.

100 Write with the Perfect Tenses

Remember: Use the present perfect, past perfect, and future perfect tenses to show how actions are related in time. Study the chart.

Tense	When Do You Use It?	Examples
Present Perfect	For actions that began in the past and are still going on	Aunt Lil **has been** my role model for years.
	For actions that happened at an unknown past time	I **have visited** her a lot.
Past Perfect	For actions completed before another past action	By the time she got her apartment, Aunt Lil **had lived** with us for two years.
Future Perfect	For actions that will happen before a future time	By the end of the month, she **will have bought** a house.

Try It

A. Complete each sentence. Write the correct perfect tense of the verb in parentheses.

1. I _____ Aunt Lil my whole life. **(know)**

2. She always _____ as a role model to me. **(serve)**

3. By the time she was thirty, she _____ medical school. **(finish)**

4. Next month, she _____ a doctor for thirty years. **(be)**

B. (5–8) Complete each sentence with a verb in the perfect tense. Use work, spend, and accomplish. You may need to use a verb more than once.

Aunt Lil _____ hard her whole life. By the time she was 22, she _____ her way through college. By the time she became a doctor, she _____ years working at a hospital. By the time I am her age, I hope I _____ as much as she has.

C. Answer the questions. Use the present perfect, the past perfect, and the future perfect tenses.

9. What have you worked hard at? I _____

_____.

10. What had you done before you turned fifteen? _____

_____

11. By the time you grow up, what will you have accomplished? _____

_____

D. (12–16) Who is your role model? Why has that person been a model to you? Write at least five sentences. Use the present perfect, the past perfect, and the future perfect tenses.

_____

_____

_____

_____

_____

Edit It

E. (17–20) Edit this letter. Fix the four perfect tense verbs.

Dear Aunt Lil,

I have almost complete my first year of medical school. Your encouragement have helped me tremendously. By the time I finish medical school, I have learned so much. You have been there to support me the whole time. I hope that one day I will be the same kind of role model for someone else like you been for me.

Love,

Juanita

Proofreader's Marks
Add text:
I had a tough semester. ^have
Change text:
Aunt Lil ~~have~~ been a great role model. ^has
See all Proofreader's Marks on page ix.

101 Can a Verb Act Like an Adjective?

Yes, When It Is a Participle

- Verbs have **four principal parts**. For example:

Present	Present Participle	Past	Past Participle
fly	flying	flew	flown
sing	singing	sang	sung

- Sometimes a **participle** is part of a verb phrase. Sometimes, however, it acts as an adjective to describe a noun or pronoun.

In spring, the birds **are singing**. The **singing** birds make nests.

Flying, the birds sing. They **are singing**.

The **singing** birds sounds pretty. **Singing**, they fly away.

Try It

A. Combine the sentences. Move the underlined participles to tell about a noun or a pronoun in the other sentence.

1. In winter, I love to watch the snow. The snow is **falling**.

   _____

2. After the snow stops, I skate on the pond. The pond is **frozen**.

   _____

3. I go home for hot chocolate. I am **refreshed**.

   _____

4. In spring, I love to see flowers. The flowers are **blooming**.

   _____

5. I see the bees pollinating them. The bees are **buzzing**.

   _____

B. Use the participle to combine the sentences.

6. In summer, I love to play in the waves at the beach. The waves are rolling.

_____

7. The seagulls try to steal my food. The seagulls are diving.

_____

8. I pack up and go home at the end of the day. I am tired.

_____

9. In autumn, I love to see the colors of the leaves on the trees. The colors are changing.

_____

Write It

C. Complete each sentence to tell something that you like to do in each season. Use a participle to describe a noun or pronoun.

10. In winter, _____

_____.

11. In spring, _____

_____.

12. In summer, _____

_____.

13. In autumn, _____

_____.

D. (14–15) Write at least two sentences about your favorite season. Tell why you like that season. Use a participle to describe a noun or pronoun in each sentence.

_____

_____

_____

_____

102 What Are Participial Phrases?

Phrases That Start with a Participle

- A **phrase** is a group of related words that does not have a subject and a predicate. A **participial phrase** begins with a present **participle** or past **participle**. It describes a noun or pronoun.

  I see people **dumping garbage into the water**.

  participial phrase

  Concerned about the pollution, I think about what I can do.

  participial phrase

- Sometimes you can combine sentences by using a participial phrase. Place the participial phrase near the word that it describes. If the phrase begins a sentence, follow it with a comma (,).

  We see the factories. They **pollute the water**.
  We see the factories **polluting the water**.

  I help keep the earth unpolluted. I am **recycling paper and plastics**.
  Recycling paper and plastics, I help keep the earth unpolluted.

Try It

A. Use a participial phrase to combine the sentences. Write the new sentence.

1. Chemicals pollute the earth. They are seeping into the ground.

   _____

2. Garbage pollutes the water. Garbage is floating in the water.

   _____

3. People endanger our forests. People are cutting down too many trees.

   _____

4. I see running water. It is dripping from the faucet.

   _____

5. People waste our water supply. They are letting their faucets drip.

   _____

B. Use a participial phrase to combine the sentences. Write each new sentence.

6. Sometimes there are oil spills. The oil spills are caused by humans.

_____

7. This bird needs help. It has been covered by oil from the spill.

_____

8. People are washing the bird. It has been rescued from the oily water.

_____

9. The water isn't safe for seals. The water has been polluted by the spill.

_____

10. This river is polluted, too. This river has been contaminated by dirty water in storm drains.

_____

11. These fish have died. They have been exposed to pollution.

_____

Write It

C. Use the participial phrases in your own sentences.

12. Tangled up in a fishing net, _____.

13. Made from plastic, _____.

14. Recycling paper, glass, and plastic, _____.

15. Thinking about a safe environment, _____.

D. (16–20) How can people help keep the environment clean? Write at least five sentences to answer this question. Use a participial phrase in each sentence.

_____

_____

_____

_____

_____

103 What Is a "Dangling Participle"?

It's a Participle That Describes the Wrong Word.

- Always place a **participial phrase** by the word it describes. Sometimes you can just move the phrase to fix the problem.

  Not OK: I see a rabbit **working in the garden**.

  OK: **Working in the garden**, I see a rabbit.

- Sometimes you need to rephrase the sentence and include a word for the participle to describe.

  Not OK: **Using a spade**, the holes are for my plants.

  OK: **Using a spade**, I dig holes for my plants.

Try It

A. Rewrite each sentence to fix the dangling participle.

1. Planting their garden, I have happy memories of my grandparents. _____

_____

2. Thinking of my grandparents' garden, it gave me the idea to plant my own garden.

_____

3. Loving cucumbers, my garden had a lot of cucumber plants. _____

_____

B. Rewrite each sentence. Add a participial phrase from the box. Punctuate the new sentences carefully.

cut into my salad	growing on the vines	wanting my plants to grow

4. I watered them every day. _____

5. I saw tiny cucumbers. _____

6. I tasted the delicious cucumbers. _____

_____

C. Answer the questions about growing food. Use a participial phrase in each answer.

7. Why do people grow their own food? _____

_____

8. How do people grow their own food? _____

_____

D. (9–12) What vegetables would you grow in your garden? Write at least four sentences. Use a participial phrase in each sentence. Check for and fix any dangling participles.

_____

_____

_____

_____

_____

_____

Edit It

E. (13–15) Edit this journal entry. Fix the three mistakes with dangling participles.

August 30

I saw one of my tomatoes turning red.

I felt very impatient. Knowing that the

tomatoes were ripening, they gave me ideas

for recipes. Being very sweet, I knew the

tomatoes would be good in a salad. Having

had such a good experience this year, there

will definitely be tomatoes next year, too.

Proofreader's Marks
Delete:
Being green, ~~I knew~~ the tomatoes were not ripe.
Change text:
Wanting fresh tomatoes, I thought about having a garden, ~~a garden came to mind.~~
See all Proofreader's Marks on page ix.

104 Can Absolutes Help Your Writing?

Absolutely!

- An **absolute** is almost a complete sentence, but it is missing a form of the word **be**. It has a subject and a participle. An absolute relates to the entire sentence after it.

  The cool breeze tickling my face, I wake up ready for the new day.
  absolute

  The sun rising on the horizon, the day will begin soon.
  absolute

- Sometimes you can use an absolute to combine sentences and make your writing more interesting. These sentences were combined to form the sentences above.

  I wake up ready for the new day. **The cool breeze is tickling my face.**

  The day will begin soon. **The sun is rising on the horizon.**

Try It

A. **Use an absolute with a present participle to combine each pair of sentences.**

1. I prepare for my hike. The mountain is calling to me. _____

_____

2. The trees glitter in the sunlight. The dew is clinging to their leaves. _____

_____

3. I begin my hike. The top of the mountain is awaiting me. _____

_____

B. **Use an absolute with a past participle to combine each pair of sentences.**

4. I enjoy the view from the mountaintop. My stomach is filled from lunch. _____

_____

5. I'm ready to hike back down. My garbage is packed in my backpack. _____

_____

C. Read the absolute. Then complete each sentence.

6. The deer foraging in the forest, _____
_____ .

7. The birds flying overhead, _____
_____ .

8. The mountain standing majestically behind me, _____
_____ .

D. (9–12) How do you show respect for places you visit? Write at least four sentences. Use an absolute in each sentence.

_____

_____

_____

_____

_____

E. (13–15) Edit this description. Fix the three mistakes with absolutes.

The campfire crackling in the background, I get ready to cook my dinner. The stars have been shining in the sky above me, I listen to the night sounds. I hear an owl hooting. Its prey is hiding below, the owl searches for its dinner. The lake is shimmering in the moonlight, the campground is quiet and peaceful.

Proofreader's Marks

Delete:

The campfire is crackling, my whole body feels warm.

See all Proofreader's Marks on page ix.

(105) Enrich Your Sentences

Remember: A **participle** is a verb form that can act as an adjective. A **participial phrase** begins with a participle. Participles and participial phrases describe nouns and pronouns.

- A **participle** ends in **-ing** or **-ed**, or it has a special form. It can stand alone, or it can come at the start of a **participial phrase**.

  Flowering gardens adorn the rooftop.

  Planting a garden on the rooftop, residents have made this building fun to live in.

  Ripened vegetables are ready to be picked.

  I'm eating the vegetables **grown by residents of our building**.

- You can use participial phrases to combine or expand sentences.

  Planted by all of us, the gardens are spectacular.

Try It

A. Use a participial phrase beginning with a present participle to combine each pair of sentences. Write the new sentence.

1. I am reading a report. The report describes the city of the future. _____

_____

2. People will have gardens. The gardens will grow on rooftops. _____

_____

3. The plants will get enough sunlight. They will be on the rooftops. _____

_____

B. Use a participial phrase beginning with a past participle to combine each pair of sentences. Write the new sentence.

4. People will not litter. They will be worried about pollution. _____

_____

5. The city will attract residents. The city will be admired for its cleanliness. _____

_____

C. Expand the sentences with participial phrases. Write the new sentences.

6. I want to move to the city. _____

_____

7. The city has a lot to offer people like me. _____

_____

D. (8–12) What would your perfect city of the future be like? Write at least five sentences. Use participial phrases in each sentence.

_____

_____

_____

_____

_____

_____

Edit It

E. (13–15) Improve this letter. Add three participial phrases that describe the underlined words.

Dear Uncle Carl,

Being someone who loves city life, I am really enjoying this city. I am spending a lot of <u>time</u>. This is a really clean city. The people here do not throw trash on the streets. It is pleasant to walk along the <u>streets</u>.

<u>I</u> am doing a lot of shopping, too!

Love,

Elizabeth

Proofreader's Marks

Add text:

Impressed by the cleanliness,

Elizabeth wants to move to this city.

See all Proofreader's Marks on page ix.